The United State Patchwork Pattern Book

50 Quilt Blocks for 50 States from "Hearth & Home" Magazine

Collected
and Edited by
Barbara Bannister
& Edna Paris Ford

Dover Publications, Inc., New York

Published in Canada by General Publishing Company, Ltd.,
30 Lesmill Road, Don Mills, Toronto, Ontario.
Published in the United Kingdom by Constable and
Company, Ltd.

This Dover edition, first published in 1976, is a collection of quilt block patterns from *Hearth & Home*
Magazine, 1907-1912. The quilt patterns, instructions,
and introduction have been especially prepared for this
edition.

Design by Shaun and Susan Johnston

International Standard Book Number: 0-486-23243-3
Library of Congress Catalog Card Number: 75-2821

Manufactured in the United States of America
Dover Publications, Inc.
180 Varick Street
New York, N. Y. 10014

Introduction

The appearance of these fifty state quilt block patterns at the time of our country's Bicentennial celebration may seem to be a carefully planned event. Actually, the juxtaposition of these two occurrences is a happy coincidence, for the search for a complete set of these interesting, old quilt patterns has taken us many years.

In 1907 the Fancywork Department of a popular farm magazine, *Hearth & Home* (Vickery Publishing Company, Augusta, Maine, 1868–1933) inaugurated a series of state quilt block patterns. Readers throughout the country were asked to contribute pieced cloth blocks to represent their respective states. The block could be an original design or simply the sender's favorite. The readers responded to this request, and pictures of the selected blocks appeared in monthly issues until the series ended in 1912.

After the 48-state quilt block series was completed, *Hearth & Home* began another series called "Outlying Possessions" (later called "U. S. Territories"). This series included blocks from such territories as the Philippines, Guam, Samoa, Alaska and Hawaii. We have taken the blocks for Alaska and Hawaii from this series to complete our present fifty-state quilt block pattern collection.

Contrary to current thinking, *Hearth & Home* did sell patterns for the quilt blocks printed in the magazine. The patterns, which cost five cents, were called *perforated diagram patterns*. They were simply full-size drawings of the blocks from which the quilt maker could trace off each patch to get the exact size of each pattern piece.

In May, 1933, publication of *Hearth & Home* ceased when the magazine was merged with *Good Stories,* another Vickery publication. Since *Hearth & Home* had been printed on low-quality newsprint that deteriorated rather rapidly, few issues are still extant. This scarcity of copies contributed to the length of time it took us to locate a complete set of quilt patterns.

When these quilt blocks were published, there was a general neglect and indifference in urban areas to the craft of quilt making. We believe that farm magazines such as *Hearth & Home* helped to keep the craft alive in the rural areas where farm women continued to develop it.

Today there is a growing interest in the American patchwork quilt. These fifty state quilt blocks are authentic, unique and patriotic in theme, and present-day quilt makers will enjoy making beautiful patchwork quilts from these heirloom patterns.

We have not specified colors for the quilt blocks, but have simply indicated light, medium and dark. All the designs will work well in red, white and blue, using red for the dark, blue print for the medium and white for the light. However, in blocks which form stars, blue might be the most appropriate color for those patches which are part of the star.

Occasionally the reader sending in the quilt block also sent along a description of the finished quilt and other miscellaneous information, and these comments are included in this edition. However, since most of the quilt blocks were originally printed without any indication as to how to finish the quilt, we have added instructions for making each block and setting each quilt. We have also indicated yardage requirements. Since the majority of fabrics suitable for quilt making come in 36-inch widths, our yardage requirements are for 36-inch fabric.

This book is a collection of quilt block patterns—not an instruction book on how to do patchwork; that subject is already well covered in numerous inexpensive books on quilt making. However, here are basic instructions for making a perfectly pieced block.

Make your pattern of heavy cardboard, sandpaper or plastic. Make this the exact size the patch is to be, after sewing is done. Mark around each pattern with a pencil, on the wrong side of the material. Since patterns in this book do not allow for seams, leave space between patterns for a seam allowance. Cut ¼″ outside this pencil line. This gives your seam allowance.

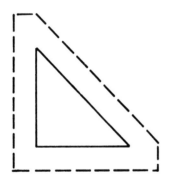

Broken line is the cutting line.
Solid line is the seam line; match to the line on the next patch. Sewing is done on this solid line.

Sew the patches together by *matching the pencil lines* and sewing along this line. If the seam allowance is not perfect, this will not show; but the *sewing line* must be perfectly straight and true, or the patches will not come together into perfectly shaped blocks. A variation of just 1/16″ on half of the patches in the quilt will add up to several inches by the time all blocks are completed and the quilt top put together.

Always make one block of any pattern before cutting patches for an entire quilt. This gives you a chance to double-check your pattern and to make sure you like both the pattern and the color choices.

If a block is said to "finish 12 inches," it means that after all of the blocks have been sewn together, the size of each block will be 12″ square. However, the completed but unjoined blocks will measure 12½″ square, the extra ¼″ all around being the seam allowance that disappears in the process of setting the blocks. If alternate plain blocks are used to set the quilt together, these plain blocks must also be cut ½″ larger than the desired finished block size.

If a quilt is put together with stripping, the strips must also be cut to allow for seams: if a strip is to finish 3″ x 72″, the strip must be cut 3½″ x 72½″. Borders must also be cut to allow for ¼″ seams.

We believe that this collection of fifty state quilt block patterns represents a crafts legacy of immense value. Today we recognize the irreplaceable contribution to our rich national heritage of the farm women who lavished their creative skills on the craft of quilt making, and we are filled with pride.

Alabama

This quilt, measuring 84 x 96 inches, is made up of fifty-six 12-inch pieced blocks set seven in width and eight in length. Bind with a bias binding of the dark material.

MATERIALS
Light, 4¼ yards
Medium (or print), 4¼ yards
Dark, 3 yards (includes bias binding)

4 Light

4 Medium

4 Medium

17 Dark

4 Light

ALLOW FOR ALL SEAMS WHEN CUTTING

Alaska

This quilt, measuring 78 x 91 inches, is made up of forty-two 13-inch pieced blocks set six in width and seven in length. Bind with dark material.

MATERIALS
Light, 2 yards
Medium, 5 yards
Dark, 3 yards (includes binding)

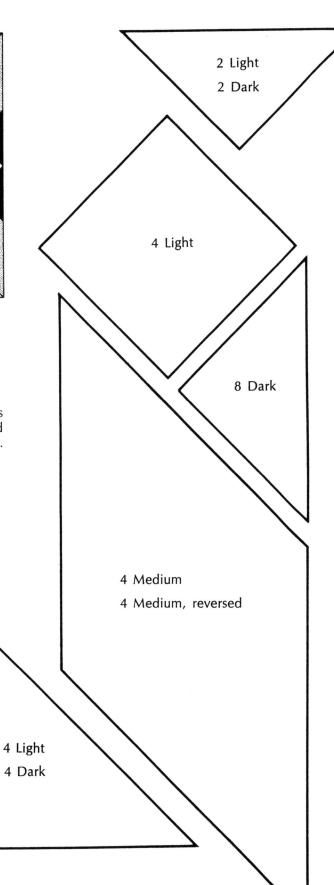

2 Light
2 Dark

4 Light

8 Dark

4 Medium
4 Medium, reversed

4 Medium

4 Light
4 Dark

ALLOW FOR ALL SEAMS WHEN CUTTING

2

Arizona

This quilt, measuring 84 x 96 inches, is made up of fifty-six 12-inch pieced blocks set seven in width and eight in length. Bind with dark material. A light and dark shade of the same color may be used, or a print and plain fabric.

MATERIALS
Light, 8 yards
Dark, 6½ yards (includes binding)

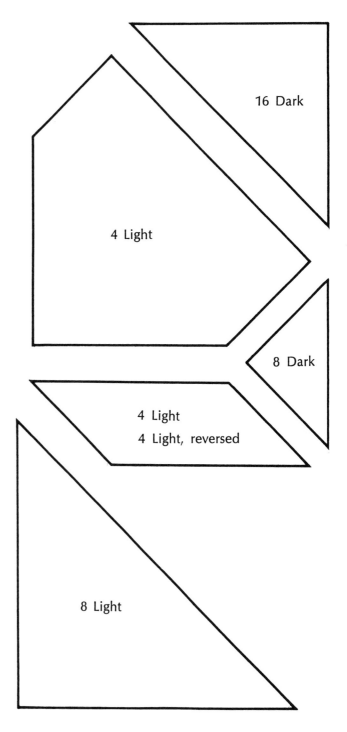

16 Dark

4 Light

8 Dark

4 Light
4 Light, reversed

8 Light

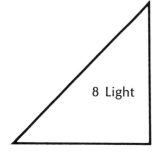

8 Light

4 Dark
4 Light

Arkansas

This quilt, measuring 84 x 108 inches, is made up of sixty-three 12-inch pieced blocks set seven in width and nine in length. Bind with dark material.

MATERIALS
Light, 5¼ yards
Medium, 4½ yards
Dark, 2¼ yards (includes binding)

4 Light

4 Dark

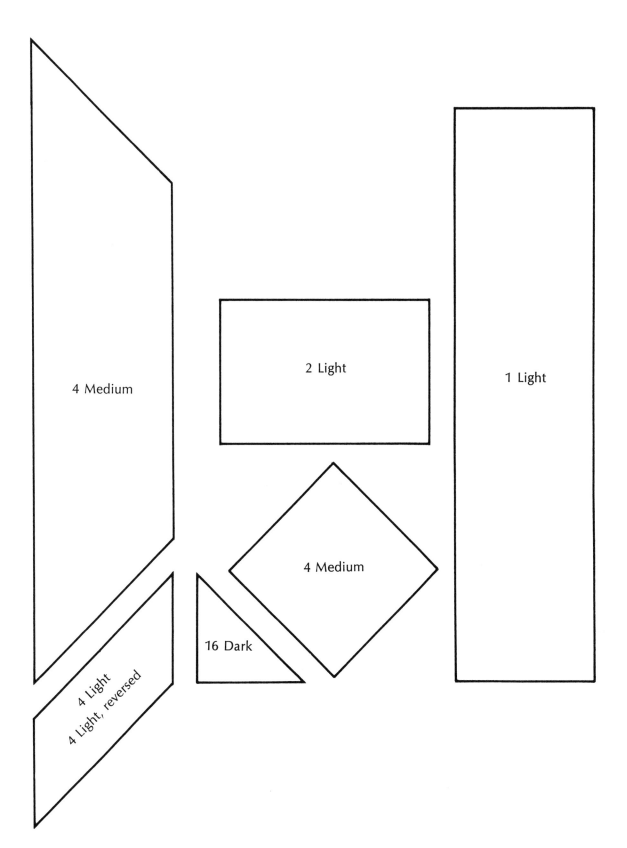

4 Medium

2 Light

1 Light

4 Medium

16 Dark

4 Light

4 Light, reversed

ALLOW FOR ALL SEAMS WHEN CUTTING

5

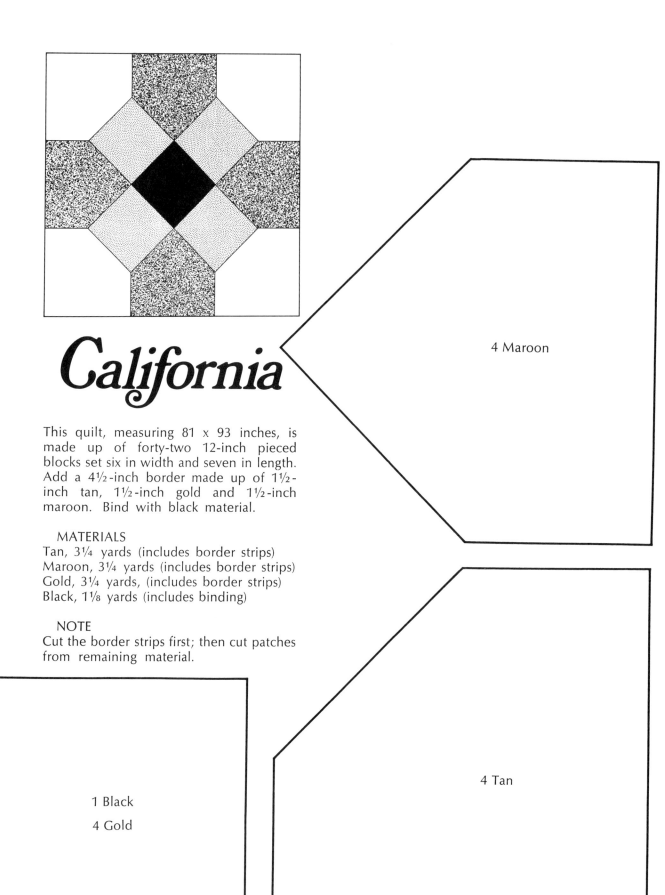

California

This quilt, measuring 81 x 93 inches, is made up of forty-two 12-inch pieced blocks set six in width and seven in length. Add a 4½-inch border made up of 1½-inch tan, 1½-inch gold and 1½-inch maroon. Bind with black material.

MATERIALS
Tan, 3¼ yards (includes border strips)
Maroon, 3¼ yards (includes border strips)
Gold, 3¼ yards, (includes border strips)
Black, 1⅛ yards (includes binding)

NOTE
Cut the border strips first; then cut patches from remaining material.

4 Maroon

4 Tan

1 Black
4 Gold

Colorado

This pattern is sometimes called "Rising Sun," although a more appropriate name would seem to be "Rising Star"! It is especially pretty made of red (or blue, yellow, or any other color preferred) with white cotton, and joined with squares or half-squares, zigzag fashion, of the same.   (Mrs. H. B. W.)

This quilt, measuring 82 x 108 inches, is made up of thirty-six pieced blocks and thirty-six plain blocks set alternately eight in width and nine in length. The blocks, which finish 10¼ x 12 inches, are set with the narrow part going across the top of the quilt.

MATERIALS
Light, 8 yards (includes plain blocks)
Dark, 2¾ yards

NOTE
Cut plain blocks first; then, cut patches from remaining material.

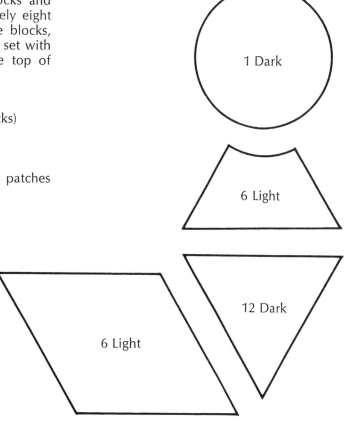

ALLOW FOR ALL SEAMS WHEN CUTTING

Continued on next page

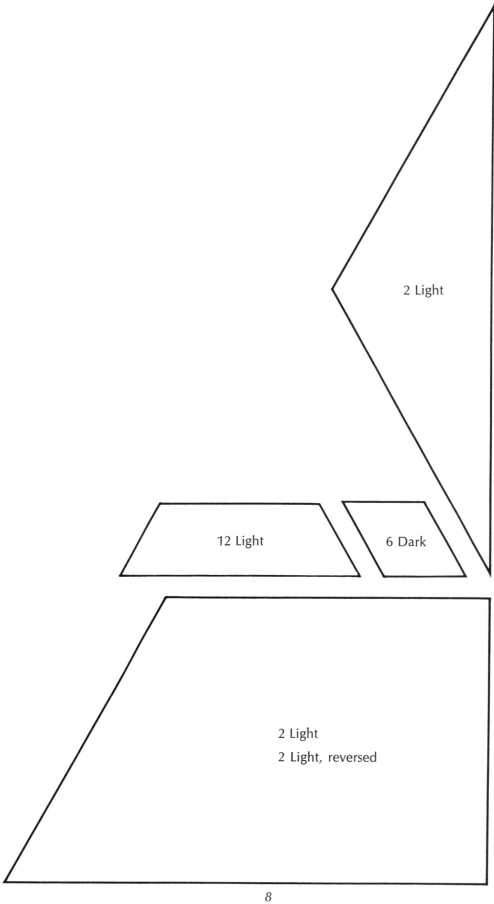

2 Light

12 Light

6 Dark

2 Light
2 Light, reversed

The "really-truly" name of this block is "Shoemaker's Puzzle." In piecing the block, if one remembers always to put the slanting side of the narrow piece onto the slanting side of the larger one, and dark to light, it is not much of a puzzle.

(Mrs. M. A. S.—Berlin, Conn.)

Connecticut

This quilt, measuring 84 x 96 inches, is made up of fifty-six 12-inch pieced blocks set seven in width and eight in length. Bind with dark material.

MATERIALS
Light, 4¾ yards
Dark, 5¼ yards

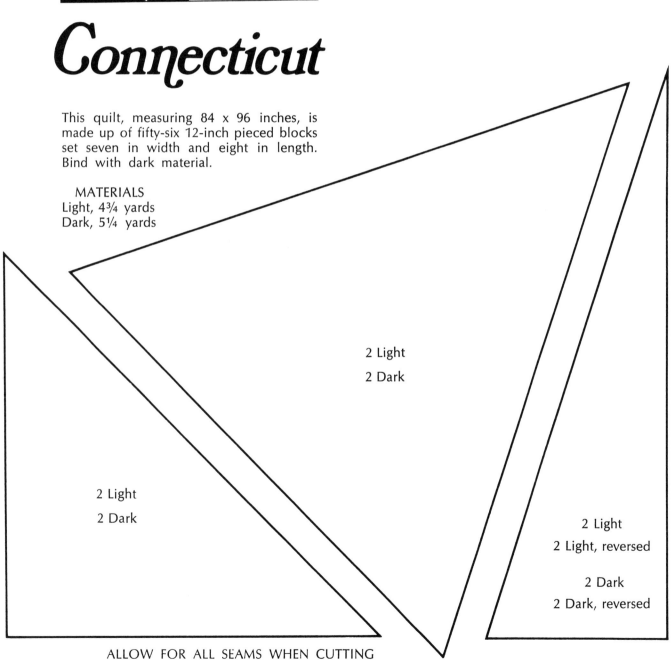

2 Light
2 Dark

2 Light
2 Dark

2 Light
2 Light, reversed

2 Dark
2 Dark, reversed

ALLOW FOR ALL SEAMS WHEN CUTTING

Delaware

This quilt, measuring 87 x 105 inches, is made up of thirty 15-inch pieced blocks set five in width and six in length with 3-inch strips set between the blocks. The strips are made up of ninety-eight A sections and sixty-nine B sections of the main block. (See diagram.) Bind with medium material.

MATERIALS
Light, 5½ yards
Medium, 3 yards (includes binding)
Dark, 4¼ yards

NOTE
Section A will finish 3 x 6 inches; section B will finish 3 x 3.

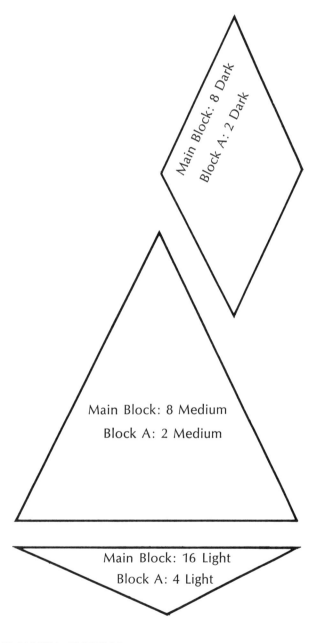

Main Block: 8 Dark
Block A: 2 Dark

Main Block: 8 Medium
Block A: 2 Medium

Main Block: 16 Light
Block A: 4 Light

Main Block: 2 Light, 2 Dark
Block B: 2 Light, 2 Dark

ALLOW FOR ALL SEAMS WHEN CUTTING

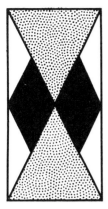

Block A

Block B

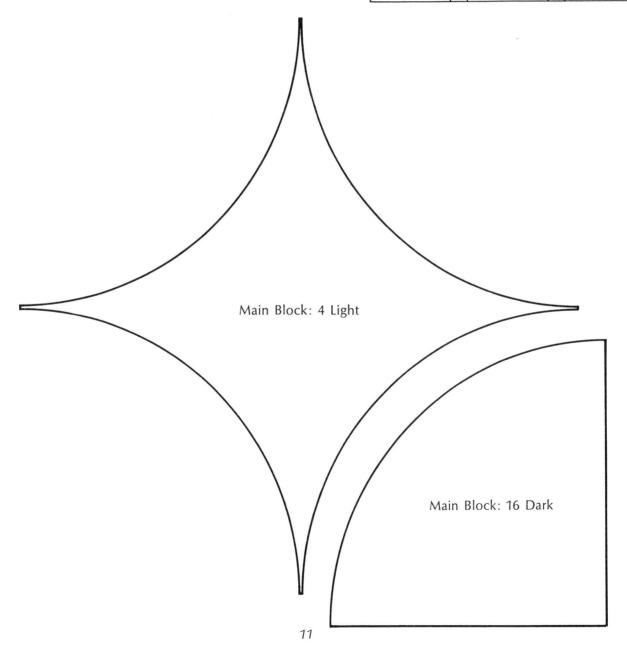

Main Block: 4 Light

Main Block: 16 Dark

Florida

This quilt, measuring 77⅝ x 90 inches, is made up of thirty-three full blocks and six half blocks. Each full block measures 15 x 17¼ inches, and the blocks are set with the wider measurement across the quilt. Set the top row with three full blocks and three half blocks in width, and the six rows in length will fall into place. The sides of the quilt are left with the pointed scallops. (See diagram.) Bind with the dark material.

MATERIALS
Light, 5¾ yards
Medium, 3½ yards
Dark, 2½ yards (including binding)

NOTE
Piece triangles first; then, sew triangles together to form the hexagon block.

Full Block: 18 Dark
Half Block: 9 Dark

Full Block: 18 Light
Half Block: 9 Light

ALLOW FOR ALL SEAMS WHEN CUTTING

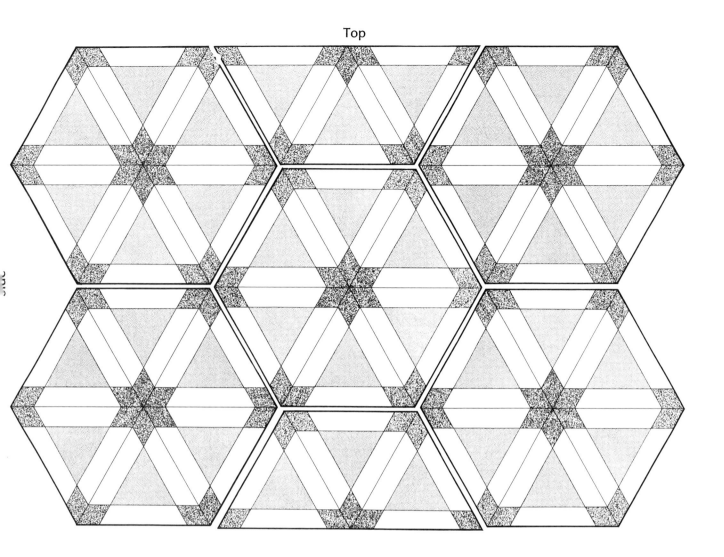

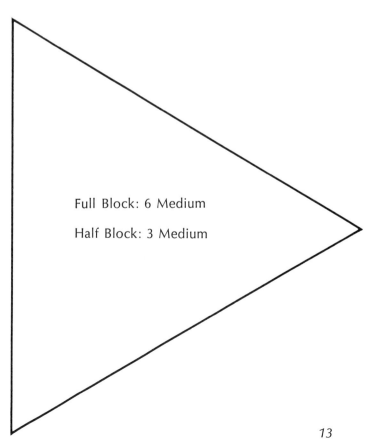

Full Block: 6 Medium

Half Block: 3 Medium

Use three colors, and join the pieced blocks with plain squares or strips or make the quilt entirely of patchwork, as you prefer. A pretty "setting" is made of half squares, the pieced block being joined corner to corner, and filled in each side with the half squares to form a straight strip; then in making the second strip arrange to have the corner of each block come halfway across the edge of a half square. This gives a zigzag setting which is very much liked by quilt makers.   (Mrs. H. B. Bates)

Georgia

This quilt, measuring 84 x 96 inches, is made up of fifty-six 12-inch pieced blocks set seven in width and eight in length. Bind with the dark material.

MATERIALS
Light, 3 yards
Medium, 4½ yards
Dark, 3 yards

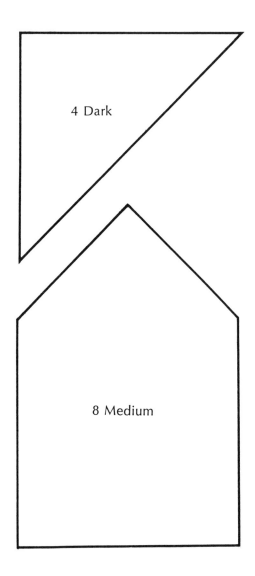

4 Dark

8 Light
4 Dark
1 Medium

8 Medium

ALLOW FOR ALL SEAMS WHEN CUTTING

14

This makes a nice album-block, and while a quilt is always prettier if uniform colors are used through-out, the design given serves admirably for utilizing scraps of two colors and white, or very light. I have designed it especially as a representative of the "Island Possessions," formerly my home.

(Mrs. Viola E. Hahn)

Hawaii

This quilt, measuring 84 x 96 inches, is made up of fifty-six 12-inch pieced blocks set seven in width and eight in length. Bind with the medium material.

MATERIALS
Light, 3¼ yards
Medium, 4 yards
Dark, 4 yards

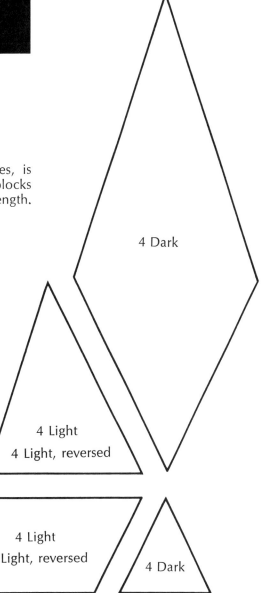

4 Dark

4 Light
4 Light, reversed

4 Light
4 Light, reversed

4 Dark

ALLOW FOR ALL SEAMS WHEN CUTTING

Continued on next page

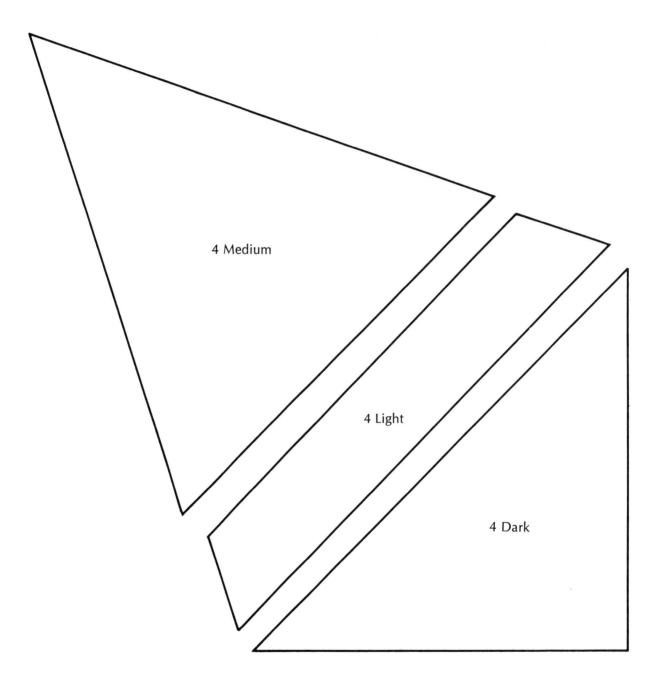

4 Medium

4 Light

4 Dark

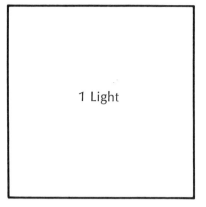

1 Light

Idaho

This quilt, measuring 84 x 108 inches, is made up of sixty-three 12-inch pieced blocks set seven in width and nine in length. Bind with medium or dark material.

MATERIALS
Light, 3½ yards
Medium, 4¾ yards
Dark, 4¾ yards

Add an additional ½ yard of medium or dark fabric for binding.

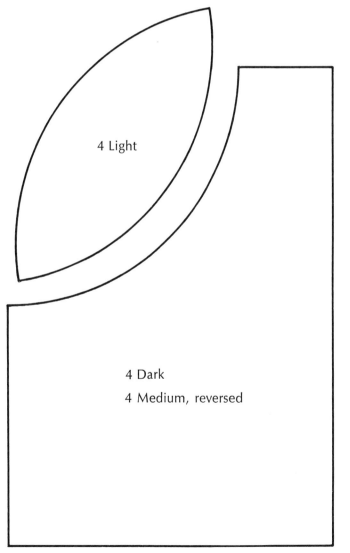

4 Light

4 Light

4 Dark
4 Medium, reversed

ALLOW FOR ALL SEAMS WHEN CUTTING

Illinois

This quilt, measuring 84 x 96 inches, is made up of fifty-six 12-inch pieced blocks set seven in width and eight in length. Bind with dark material.

MATERIALS
Light, 5 yards
Dark, 5 yards (includes binding)

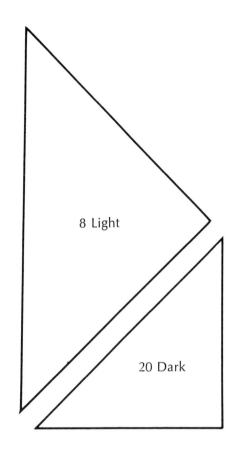

8 Light

20 Dark

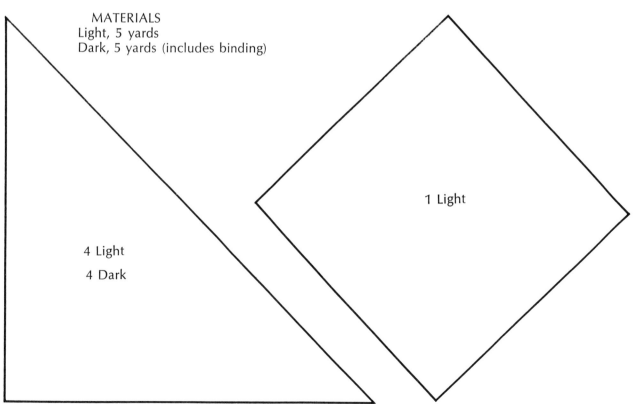

4 Light

4 Dark

1 Light

ALLOW FOR ALL SEAMS WHEN CUTTING

Indiana

This quilt, measuring 88 x 100 inches, is made up of fifty-six 12-inch pieced blocks set seven in width and eight in length. Add a 2-inch border of the dark material.

MATERIALS
Light, 8 2/3 yards
Dark, 8½ yards (includes border)

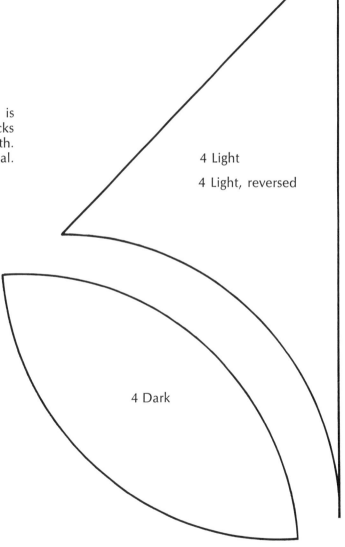

4 Light
4 Light, reversed

4 Dark

ALLOW FOR ALL SEAMS WHEN CUTTING

Continued on next page

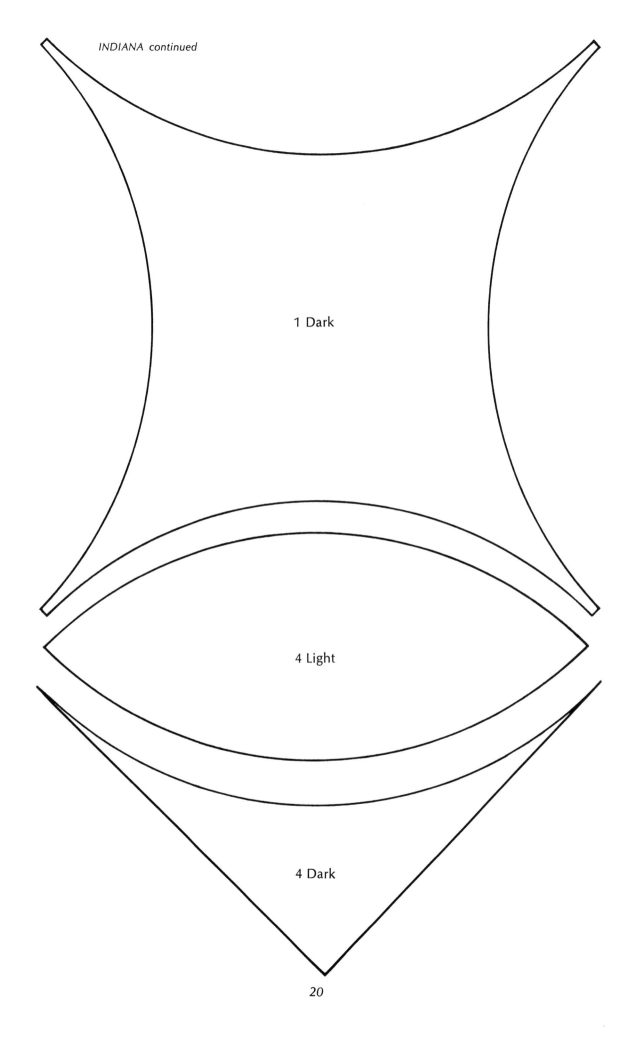

1 Dark

4 Light

4 Dark

Iowa

This quilt, measuring 84 x 96 inches, is made up of fifty-six 12-inch pieced blocks set seven in width and eight in length.

MATERIALS
Light, 7 yards
Dark, 5 yards

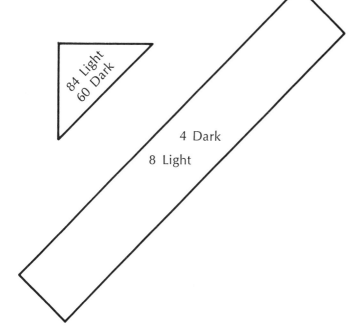

84 Light
60 Dark

4 Dark
8 Light

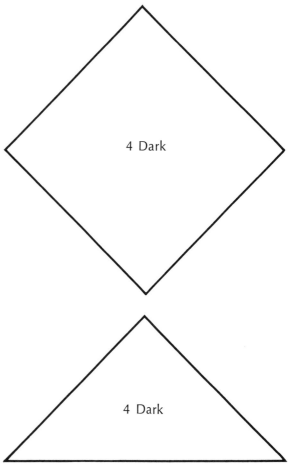

4 Dark

4 Dark

1 Light

ALLOW FOR ALL SEAMS WHEN CUTTING

Kansas

This quilt, measuring 88 x 100 inches, is made up of fifty-six 12-inch pieced blocks set seven in width and eight in length. Add a 2-inch dark border and bind with the medium shade.

MATERIALS
Light, 3½ yards
Medium, 4¾ yards (includes binding)
Dark, 4½ yards (includes border)

Made of three colors, any desired, this is a very pretty block. May be joined with plain squares, strips, or half squares to give the popular "fence rail" setting.
(Sunflower Sue)

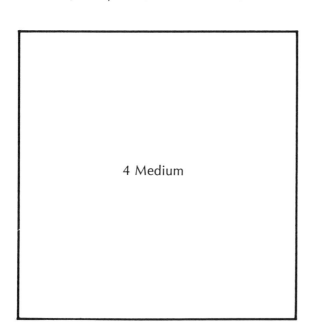

4 Medium

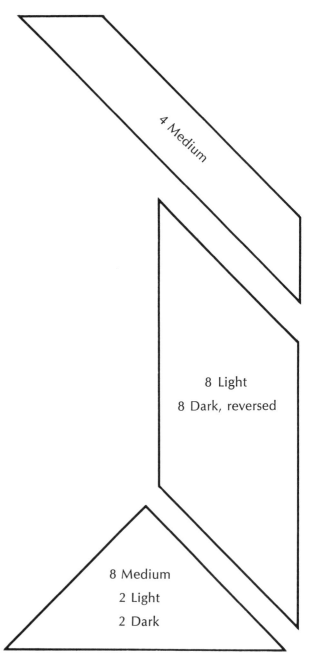

4 Medium

8 Light
8 Dark, reversed

8 Medium
2 Light
2 Dark

ALLOW FOR ALL SEAMS WHEN CUTTING

Kentucky

This quilt, measuring 93¼ x 103 inches, is made up of sixty-three 11 x 12¾-inch pieced blocks set seven in width and nine in length with the wider measurement going across the quilt. Add a 2-inch border and a binding of the dark material.

MATERIALS
Light (or white), 7¼ yards
Dark (or color), 5¼ yards (includes border and binding)

NOTE
Cut the border strips first; then cut patches from the remaining material.

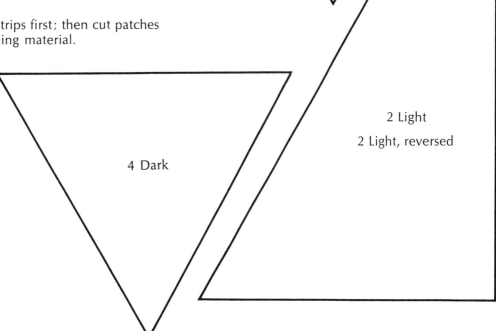

8 Light
2 Dark

2 Light
2 Light, reversed

4 Dark

ALLOW FOR ALL SEAMS WHEN CUTTING

This is a very desirable pattern for a church album-quilt—since each block may contain four names. The quilt may be all of pieced blocks, or set by means of plain strips or squares. A very pretty quilt was made of red, white and blue, the four large half squares of the latter color, and joined together with narrow strips of blue. (L. L. H.—Shreveport, La.)

Louisiana

This quilt, measuring 94 x 107 inches, is made up of fifty-six 12-inch pieced blocks set seven in width and eight in length with 1-inch dark (or blue) strips set between the blocks. Finish with a 2-inch border of the dark color.

MATERIALS
Light (or white), 3¼ yards
Medium (or red), 2¼ yards
Dark (or blue), 5½ yards (includes 1-inch strips and 2-inch border)

NOTE
Cut the border and strips first; cut patches from the remaining material.

4 Light

4 Dark

8 Medium

ALLOW FOR ALL SEAMS WHEN CUTTING

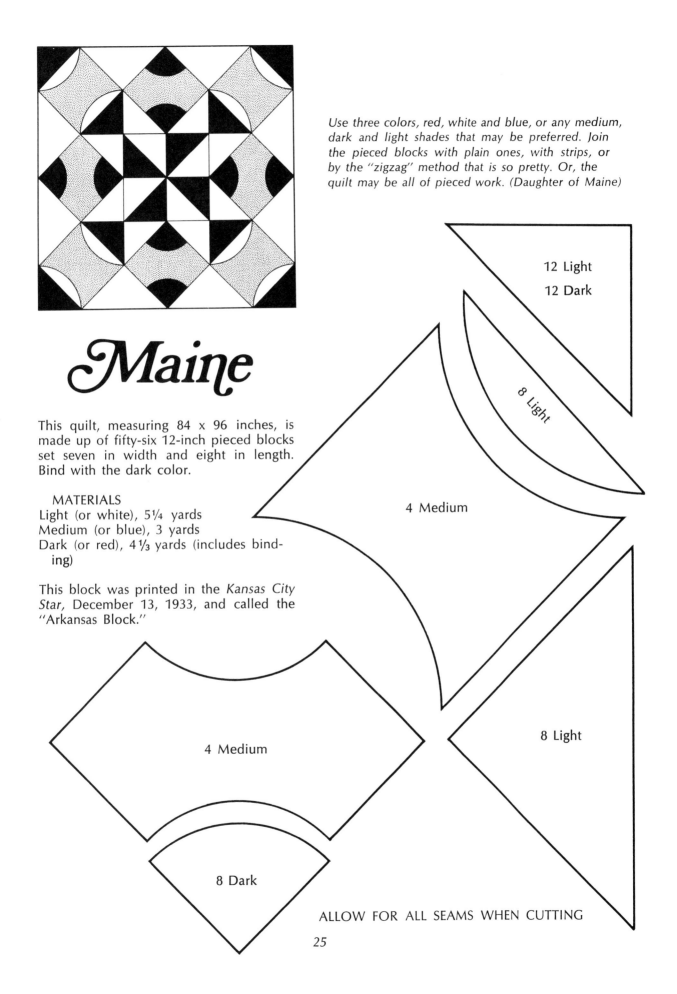

Use three colors, red, white and blue, or any medium, dark and light shades that may be preferred. Join the pieced blocks with plain ones, with strips, or by the "zigzag" method that is so pretty. Or, the quilt may be all of pieced work. (Daughter of Maine)

Maine

This quilt, measuring 84 x 96 inches, is made up of fifty-six 12-inch pieced blocks set seven in width and eight in length. Bind with the dark color.

MATERIALS
Light (or white), 5¼ yards
Medium (or blue), 3 yards
Dark (or red), 4⅓ yards (includes binding)

This block was printed in the *Kansas City Star*, December 13, 1933, and called the "Arkansas Block."

12 Light
12 Dark

8 Light

4 Medium

4 Medium

8 Light

8 Dark

ALLOW FOR ALL SEAMS WHEN CUTTING

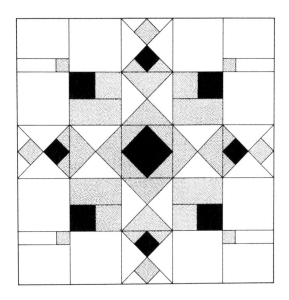

Maryland

This quilt, measuring 81 x 96 inches, is made up of thirty 15-inch pieced blocks set five in width and six in length. Add a 3-inch border of the medium material and bind with the dark material.

MATERIALS
Light, 5¾ yards
Medium, 3¾ yards (includes border)
Dark, 2 yards (includes binding)

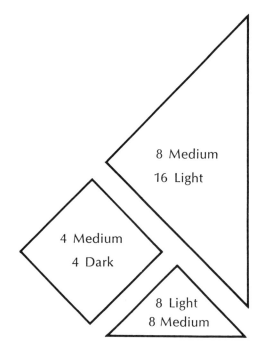

8 Medium
16 Light

4 Medium
4 Dark

8 Light
8 Medium

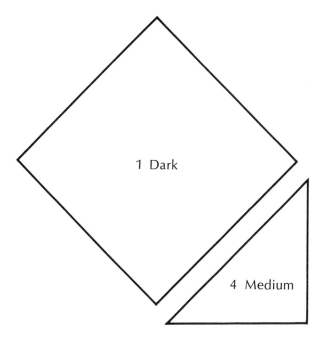

1 Dark

4 Medium

ALLOW FOR ALL SEAMS WHEN CUTTING

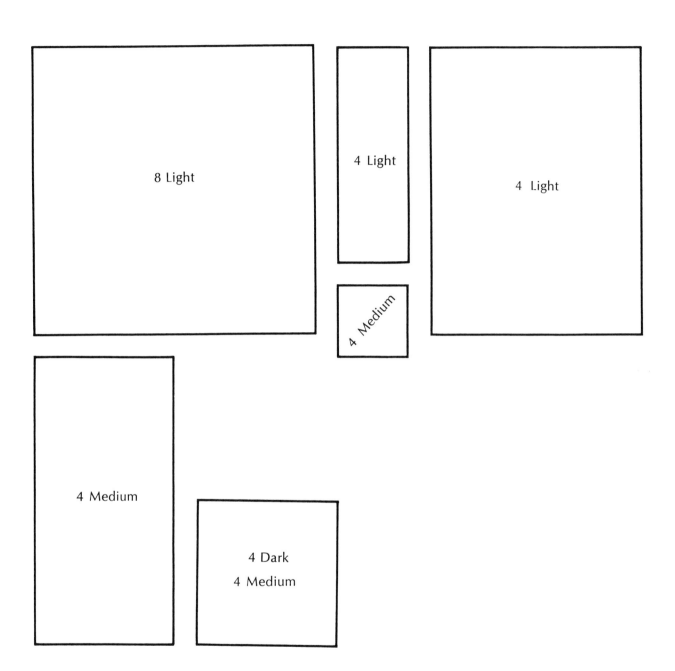

8 Light

4 Light

4 Light

4 Medium

4 Medium

4 Dark

4 Medium

This block serves admirably to use small pieces of dark and light calico, gingham or other cotton goods. It also makes a very pretty album quilt-block, the name and address of the friend who pieces it, or who furnishes scraps of her dresses to make it, being written on the white strip surrounding the center. It may be joined in any way desired. I joined my quilt by means of a white strip outside the pieced block as illustrated, one strip serving to join two blocks.   (Mrs. T.W.F.—Taunton, Mass.)

Massachusetts

This quilt, measuring 86 x 100 inches, is made up of forty-two 12-inch pieced blocks set six in width and seven in length with 2-inch strips between the blocks and a two inch border of the light fabric all around. Bind with dark material.

MATERIALS
Light, 5½ yards (includes strips and
  border)
Dark, 3½ yards (includes binding)

4 Light

56 Light
56 Dark

4 Light
4 Dark

ALLOW FOR ALL SEAMS WHEN CUTTING

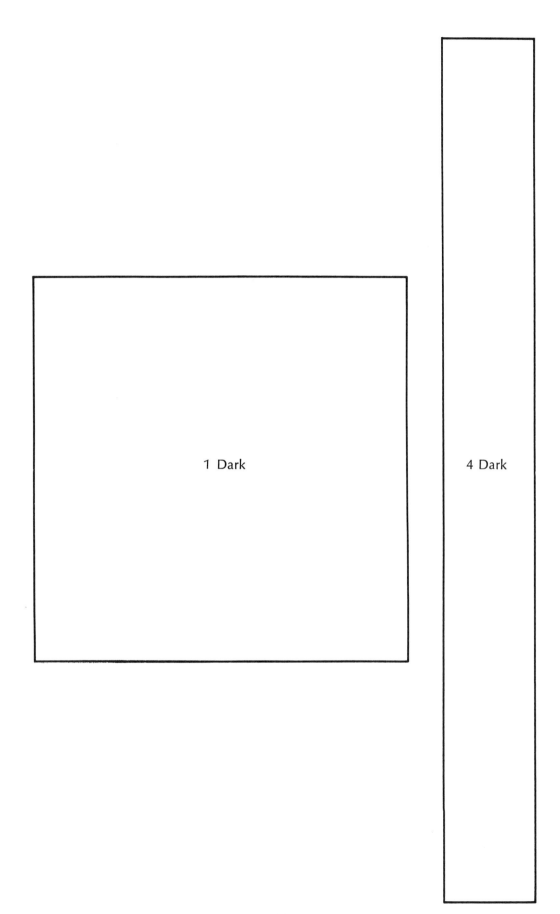

1 Dark

4 Dark

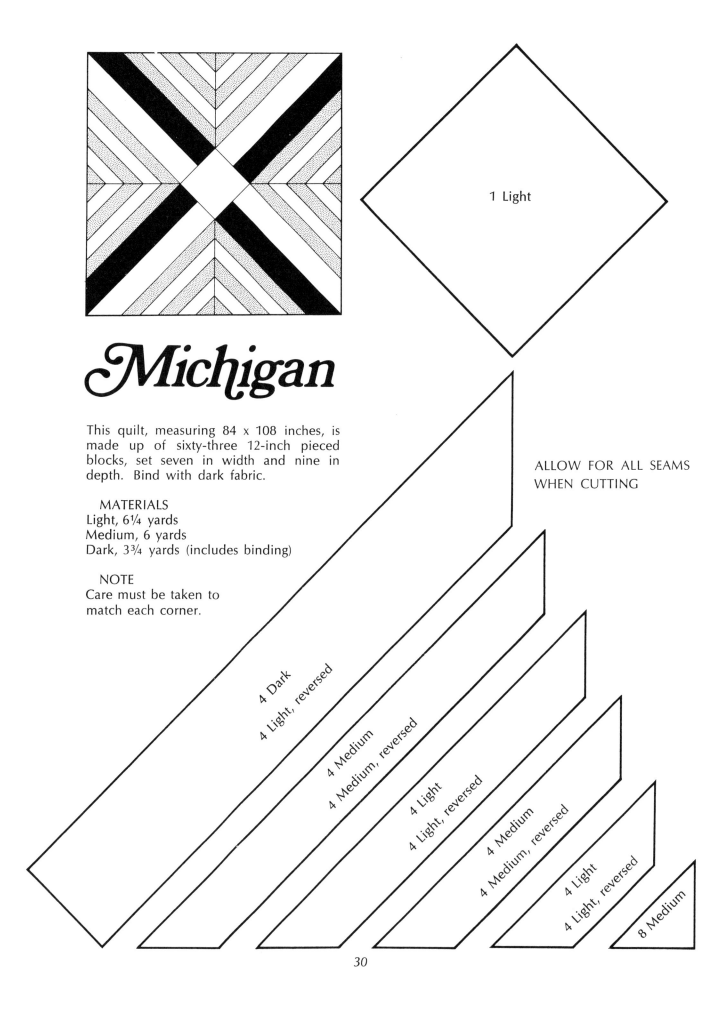

Michigan

This quilt, measuring 84 x 108 inches, is made up of sixty-three 12-inch pieced blocks, set seven in width and nine in depth. Bind with dark fabric.

MATERIALS
Light, 6¼ yards
Medium, 6 yards
Dark, 3¾ yards (includes binding)

NOTE
Care must be taken to match each corner.

1 Light

ALLOW FOR ALL SEAMS WHEN CUTTING

4 Dark
4 Light, reversed

4 Medium
4 Medium, reversed

4 Light
4 Light, reversed

4 Medium
4 Medium, reversed

4 Light
4 Light, reversed

8 Medium

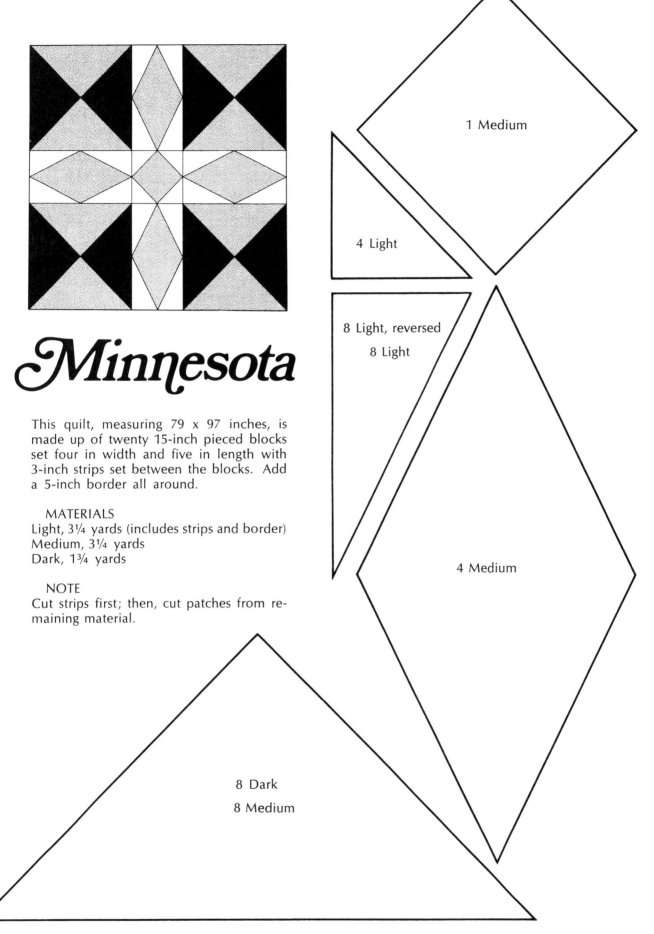

Minnesota

This quilt, measuring 79 x 97 inches, is made up of twenty 15-inch pieced blocks set four in width and five in length with 3-inch strips set between the blocks. Add a 5-inch border all around.

MATERIALS
Light, 3¼ yards (includes strips and border)
Medium, 3¼ yards
Dark, 1¾ yards

NOTE
Cut strips first; then, cut patches from remaining material.

1 Medium

4 Light

8 Light, reversed
8 Light

4 Medium

8 Dark
8 Medium

ALLOW FOR ALL SEAMS WHEN CUTTING

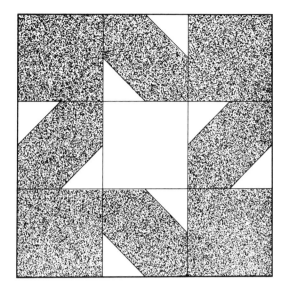

Mississippi

This quilt, measuring 84 x 96 inches, is made up of fifty-six 12-inch pieced blocks set seven in width and eight in length.

MATERIALS
Light, 3¾ yards
Dark, 7¼ yards

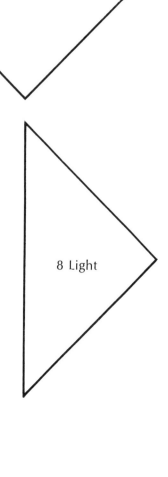

4 Dark

4 Dark

1 Light

8 Light

ALLOW FOR ALL SEAMS WHEN CUTTING

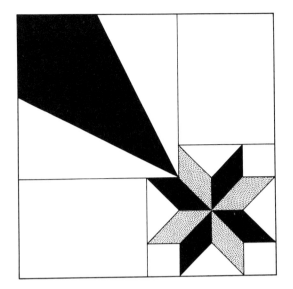

Missouri

This quilt, measuring 84 x 108 inches, is made up of thirty-two 12-inch pieced blocks and thirty-one 12-inch plain blocks (cut 12½ inches) set alternately seven in width and nine in length. Bind with dark material.

MATERIALS
Light, 7½ yards (includes plain blocks)
Medium, 1¼ yards
Dark, 5 yards (includes binding)

The block may be pieced of yellow and white or yellow and blue, having the star and trail of yellow, the background white or blue, as preferred. Join the blocks according to fancy, making the quilt entirely of pieced work or with strips of plain squares or half squares. The design was originated to commemorate the return of "Halley's Comet."

(Mrs. Mamie Privett)

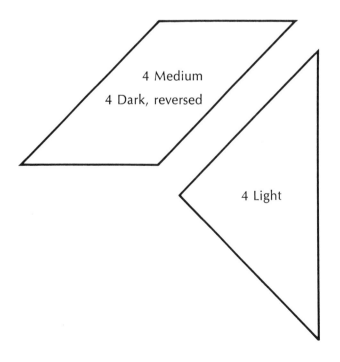

3 Light

4 Medium
4 Dark, reversed

4 Light

ALLOW FOR ALL SEAMS WHEN CUTTING

Continued on next page

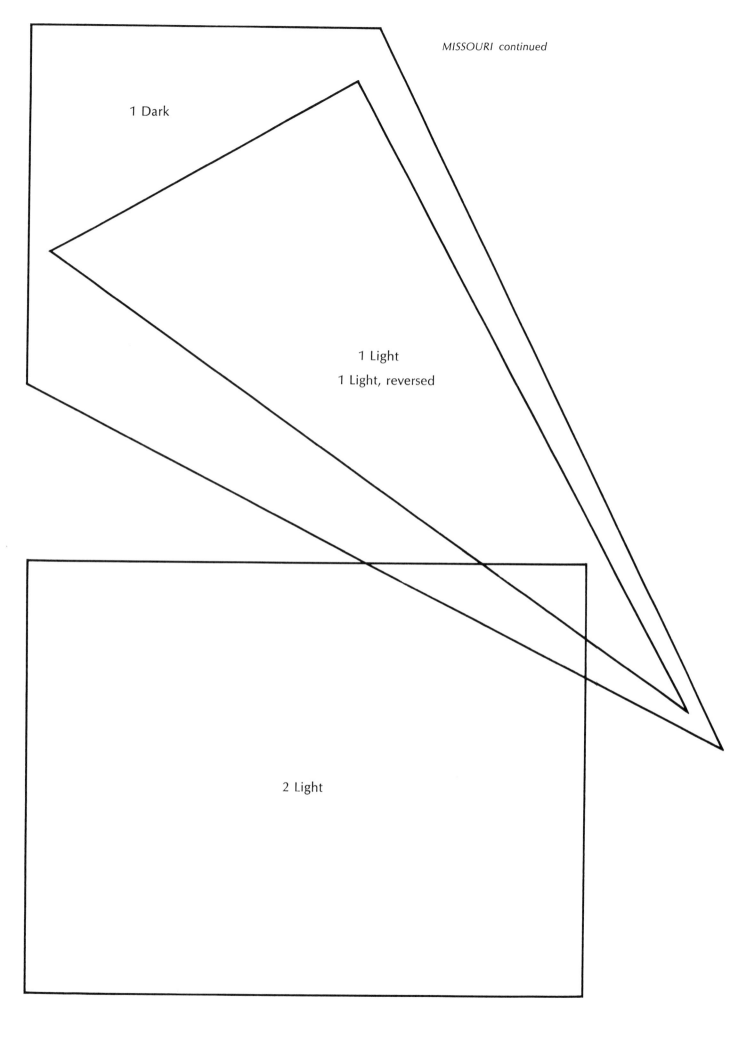

1 Dark

1 Light

1 Light, reversed

2 Light

Montana

This quilt, measuring 72 x 84 inches, is made up of forty-two 12-inch octagon-shaped pieced blocks set six in width and seven in length. The quilt is set with 30 whole stars, 22 half-stars and 4 quarter-stars, all of the medium material, filling the spaces between the octagons and creating the corners and sides. Bind with dark material.

MATERIALS
Light, 3½ yards
Medium, 4½ yards
Dark, 3¼ yards

NOTE
A larger quilt can be made by adding more blocks or adding a border of the medium material.

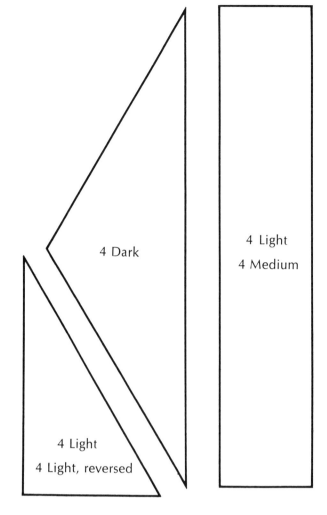

4 Dark

4 Light
4 Medium

4 Light
4 Light, reversed

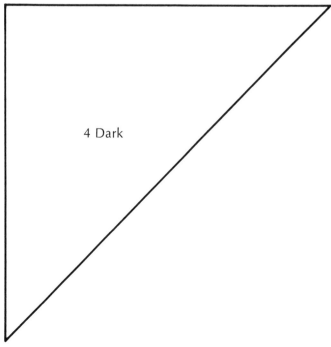

4 Dark

4 Light
5 Medium

ALLOW FOR ALL SEAMS WHEN CUTTING

Continued on next page

PATCHES FOR STARS

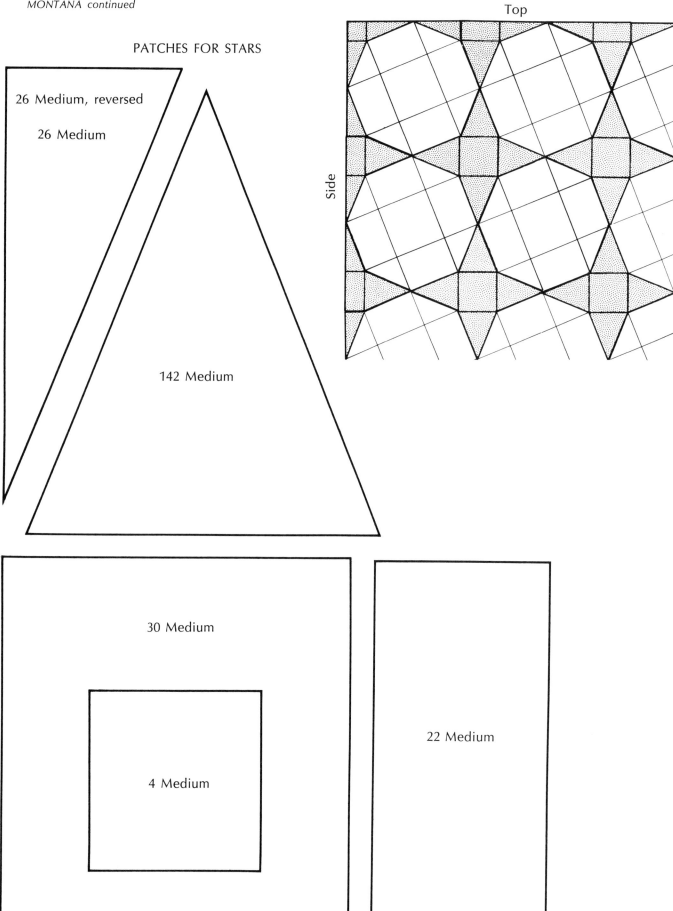

26 Medium, reversed

26 Medium

142 Medium

30 Medium

4 Medium

22 Medium

Top

Side

Nebraska

This quilt, measuring 88 x 100 inches, is made up of fifty-six 12-inch pieced blocks set seven in width and eight in length with a 2-inch border of the dark material.

MATERIALS
Light, 6⅓ yards
Medium, 1 yard
Dark, 4½ yards (includes border)

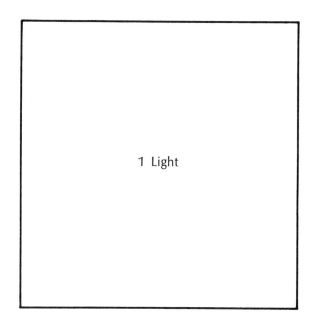

1 Light

4 Light   4 Medium   4 Dark

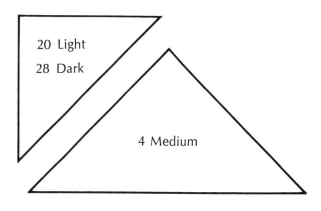

20 Light
28 Dark

4 Medium

4 Light

32 Light

40 Dark

16 Light
8 Dark

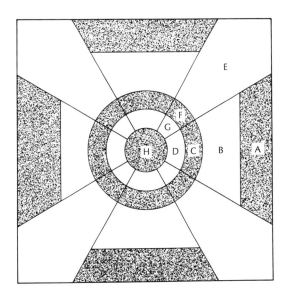

Nevada

This quilt, measuring 88 x 100 inches, is made up of fifty-six 12-inch pieced blocks set seven in width and eight in length with a 2-inch dark border.

MATERIALS
Light, 5 yards
Dark, 3 yards (includes border)

NOTE
Cut border strips first; then cut patches from remaining material.

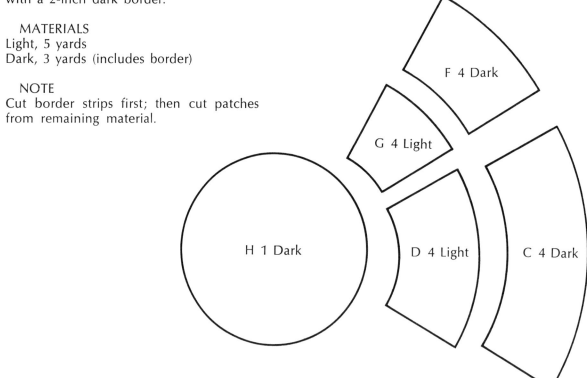

ALLOW FOR ALL SEAMS WHEN CUTTING

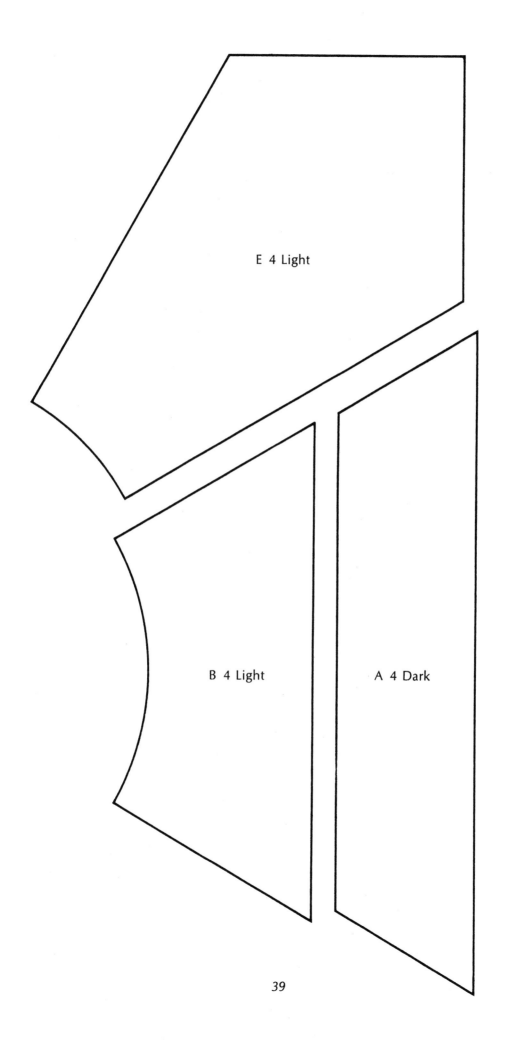

E 4 Light

B 4 Light

A 4 Dark

39

New Hampshire

This quilt, measuring 75 x 107⅝ inches, is made up of thirty-six 15 x 17¼-inch pieced blocks and eight half blocks (7½ x 17¼ inches) set five in width and eight in length. The longer measurement is set in the length, and the half blocks are used to fill in the sides of the quilt. The ends are left with the pointed scallops. (See diagram.) Bind with the medium material.

MATERIALS
Light, 4¾ yards
Medium, 2½ yards (includes binding)
Dark, 4¾ yards

NOTE
Piece triangles; then, sew triangles together to form hexagon.

Full Block: 3 Light 3 Dark

Half Block: 1 Light 2 Dark

ALLOW FOR ALL SEAMS WHEN CUTTING

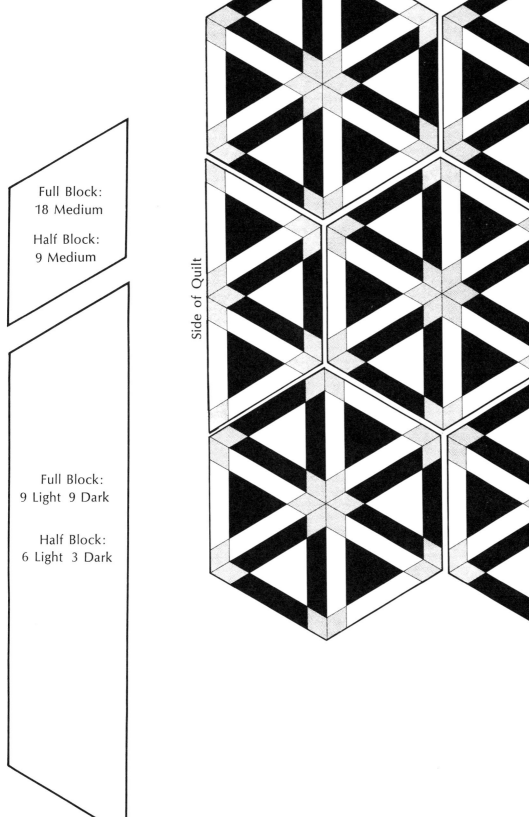

Side of Quilt

Full Block:
18 Medium

Half Block:
9 Medium

Full Block:
9 Light 9 Dark

Half Block:
6 Light 3 Dark

New Jersey

This quilt, measuring 84 x 108 inches, is made up of thirty-two 12-inch pieced blocks and thirty-one 12-inch plain blocks (cut 12½″) set alternately seven in width and nine in length. Bind with dark material.

MATERIALS
Light, 5¾ yards (includes plain blocks)
Medium, 1¾ yards
Dark, 3½ yards (includes binding)

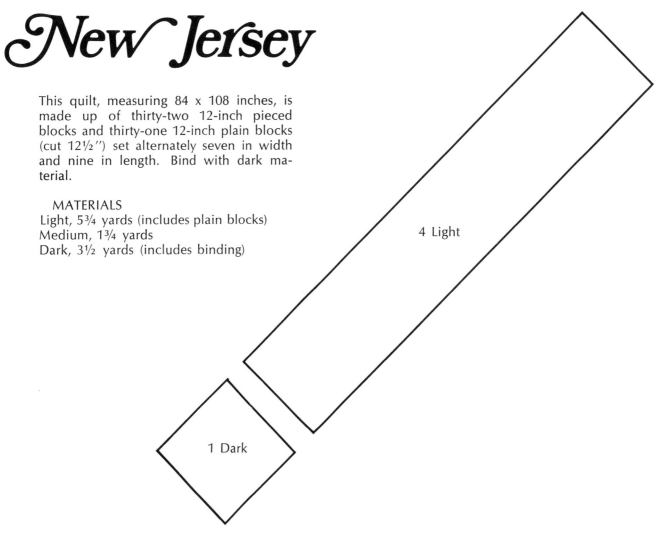

4 Light

1 Dark

ALLOW FOR ALL SEAMS WHEN CUTTING

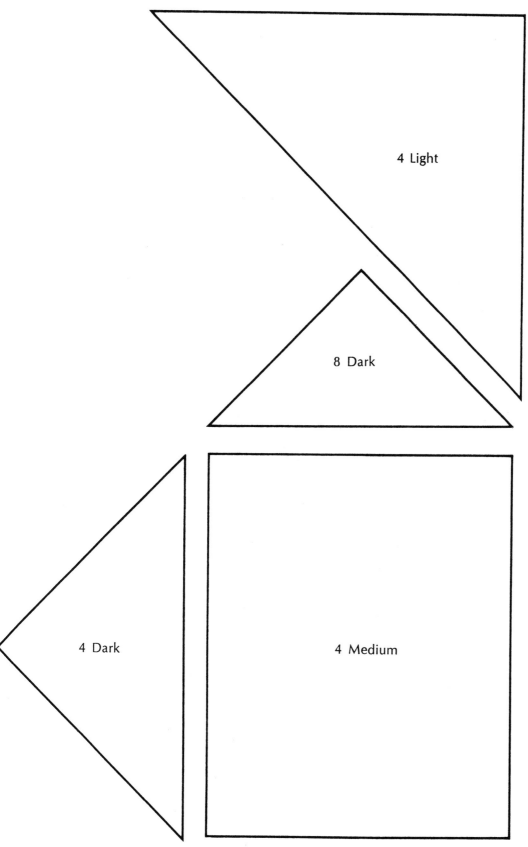

4 Light

8 Dark

4 Dark

4 Medium

New Mexico

This quilt, measuring 81 x 96 inches, is made up of thirty 15-inch pieced blocks set five in width and six in length. Add a 3-inch border of the dark material.

MATERIALS
Light, 5 yards
Dark, 8½ yards (includes border)

12 Dark
12 Light

5 Dark

16 Light
20 Dark

8 Light
4 Dark

ALLOW FOR ALL SEAMS WHEN CUTTING

New York

This quilt, measuring 84 x 108 inches, is made up of thirty-two 12-inch pieced blocks and thirty-one 12-inch plain blocks (cut 12½") set alternately seven in width and nine in length. Bind with the dark material.

MATERIALS
Light (or white), 7 yards (includes plain block)
Medium (or red), 3 yards
Dark (or blue), 2½ yards (includes binding)

NOTE
Cut plain blocks first; then cut patches from the remaining material.

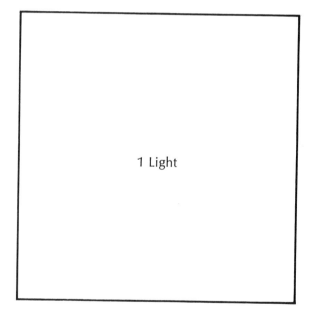

1 Light

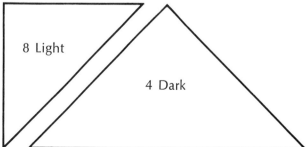

4 Dark

8 Light

4 Dark

ALLOW FOR ALL SEAMS WHEN CUTTING

45

Continued on next page

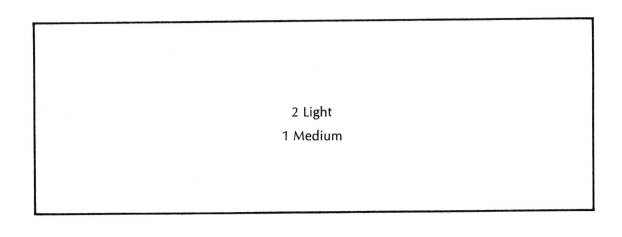

2 Light

1 Medium

1 Light

2 Medium

Place on fold of fabric

Made of three colors, with the star of yellow, this is a particularly pretty block. It makes an attractive album-block, also, the name of a friend being outlined in one white section, town and state in the second and third, and date in the fourth. It may be preferred to have the portions that show black and white (striped) in the design, of white, with the white portions striped. This will give a block with the edge of white or light. The quilt may be joined with plain squares or strips, or plain half-squares in "zigzag" fashion; or, if desired, it may be entirely of pieced blocks. (Mrs. J. L. Peters)

North Carolina

This quilt, measuring 84 x 108 inches, is made up of thirty-two 12-inch pieced blocks and thirty-one 12-inch plain blocks (cut 12½") set alternately seven in width and nine in length. Bind with dark material.

MATERIALS
Light, 6 yards (includes plain blocks)
Medium, 2 yards
Dark, 3½ yards (includes binding)

NOTE
Cut plain blocks first; cut patches from remaining material.

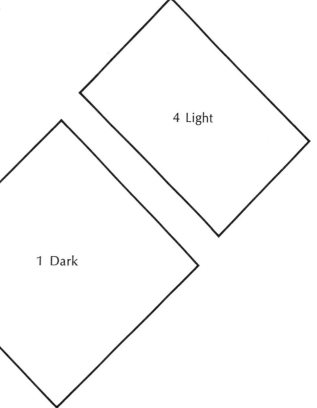

4 Light

1 Dark

ALLOW FOR ALL SEAMS WHEN CUTTING

Continued on next page

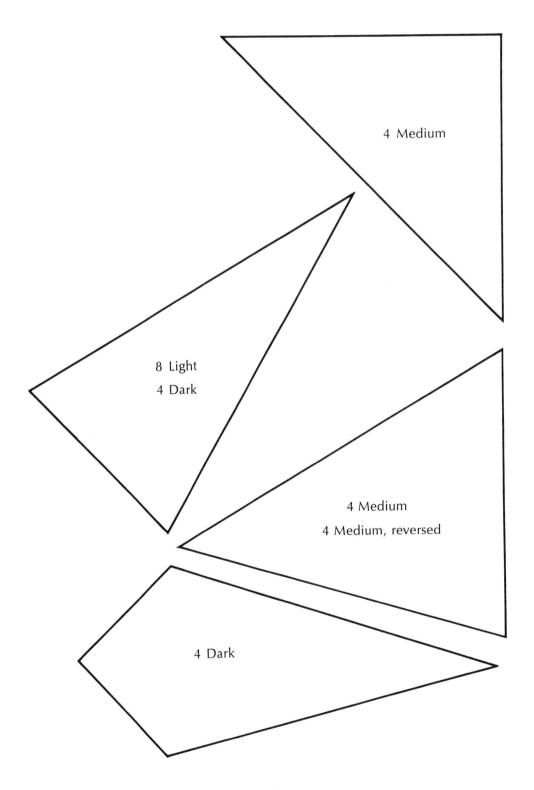

North Dakota

This quilt, measuring 89 x 106 inches, is made up of thirty 12-inch pieced blocks and twenty 12-inch plain blocks (cut 12½") set diagonally five pieced blocks in width and six pieced blocks in length. The sides and the ends of the quilt are filled with eighteen triangles, 17 inches at the base and 12 inches at the sides (cut 17½" x 12½" x 12½"). Four triangles, 12 inches at the base and 8½ inches at the sides (cut 12½" x 9" x 9") make up the four corners. Add a 2-inch border of the medium material and bind with the dark material. (See diagram.)

MATERIALS
Light, 3⅞ yards
Medium, 3 yards (includes border)
Dark, 3¼ yards (includes binding)

NOTE
If the bases of the triangles are cut on the straight of the material, the quilt will look better.

ALLOW FOR ALL SEAMS WHEN CUTTING

49

Continued on next page

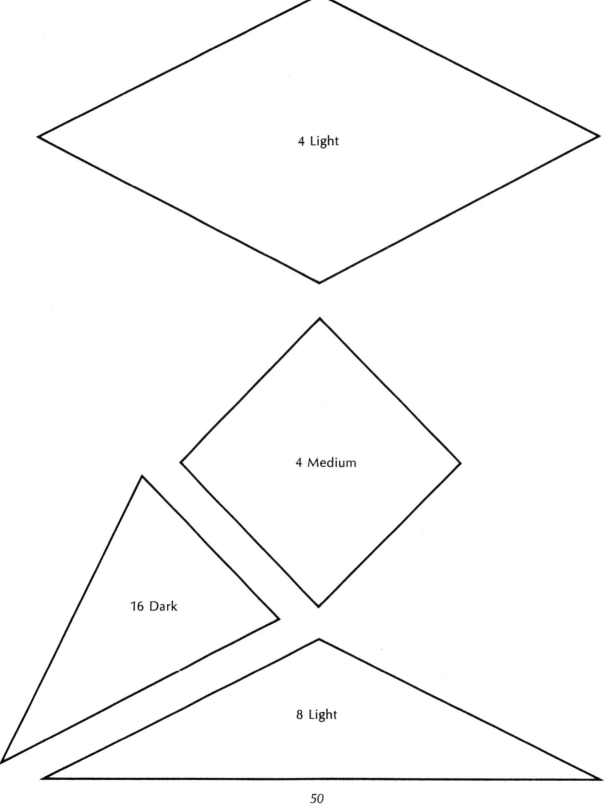

Ohio

This quilt, measuring 88 x 100 inches, is made up of fifty-six 12-inch pieced blocks set seven in width and eight in length with a 2-inch dark border.

MATERIALS
Light, 9½ yards
Medium, 2¾ yards
Dark, 3¾ yards (includes border)

NOTE
This block is made up of four small 6-inch blocks. If desired, the patches may be pieced together and appliquéd on a 12-inch square (cut 12½''), or each 6-inch square may be appliquéd separately and the four squares sewn together.

After the 12-inch square is completed, appliqué the stem onto the block. The stem may be cut from narrow fold bias tape or strips of material about ⅜-inch wide, allowing for ⅛-inch turn under.

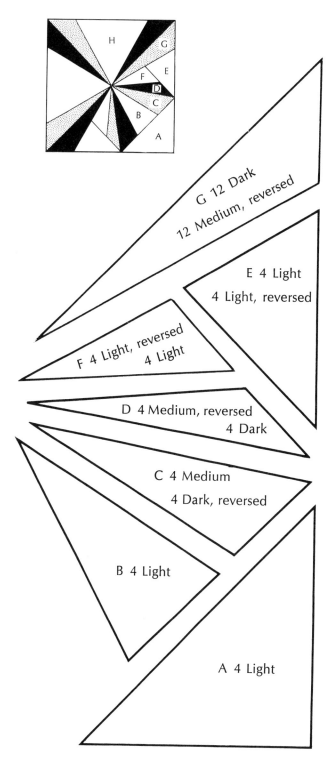

ALLOW FOR ALL SEAMS WHEN CUTTING

51

Continued on next page

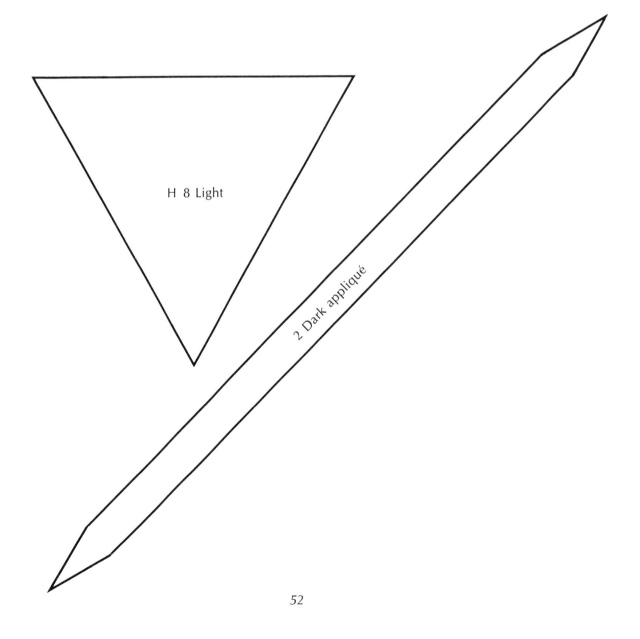

H 8 Light

2 Dark appliqué

Oklahoma

This quilt, measuring 80 x 96 inches, is made up of thirty 16-inch pieced blocks set five in width and six in length.

MATERIALS
Dark, 6½ yards
Light, 6½ yards

NOTE
Make ¼ of the block at a time, adding the outside corner to each section last; then put the block together. Cut the large, curved corner pieces first, and then cut the rest of the patches from the remaining material.

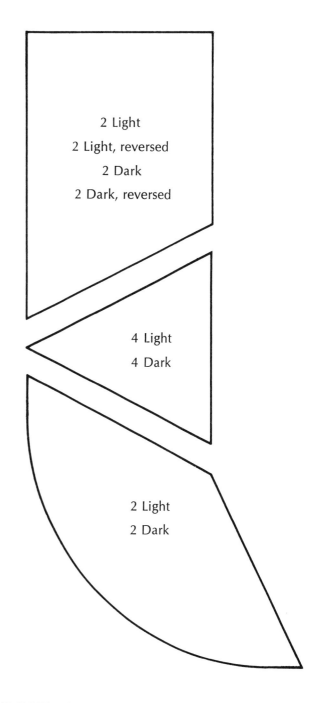

2 Light
2 Light, reversed
2 Dark
2 Dark, reversed

4 Light
4 Dark

2 Light
2 Dark

ALLOW FOR ALL SEAMS WHEN CUTTING

Continued on next page

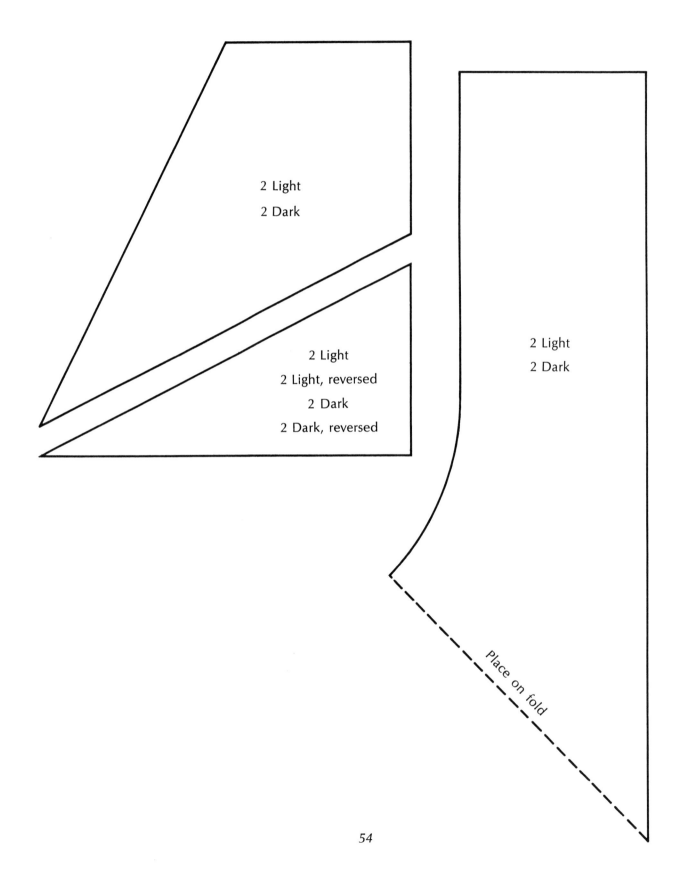

2 Light

2 Dark

2 Light

2 Light, reversed

2 Dark

2 Dark, reversed

2 Light

2 Dark

Place on fold

Oregon

This original block may be pieced of two colors—in which it will, of course, be prettiest—or any pieces of light and dark may be utilized. The blocks may be joined with alternating plain squares, or "sashed" together with strips; or, if preferred, the quilt may be entirely of pieced work.

(Mrs. N. S.—Mayville, Oregon)

This quilt, measuring 88 x 100 inches, is made up of fifty-six 12-inch pieced blocks set seven in width and eight in length with a 2-inch border of the dark material.

MATERIALS
Light, 7½ yards
Dark, 4½ yards (includes border)

4 Dark

2 Dark

ALLOW FOR ALL SEAMS WHEN CUTTING

Continued on next page

2 Light

2 Light
2 Light, reversed

2 Light
5 Dark

Pennsylvania

This quilt, measuring 78 x 90 inches, is made up of forty-two 12-inch pieced blocks set six in width and seven in length with a 3-inch border of the medium material. Bind with dark material.

MATERIALS
Light, 3½ yards
Medium, 3¼ yards (includes border)
Dark, 2½ yards (includes binding)

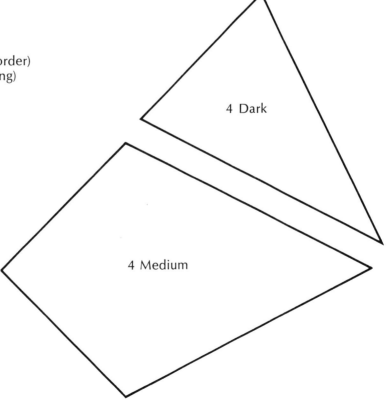

4 Dark

4 Medium

ALLOW FOR ALL SEAMS WHEN CUTTING

Continued on next page

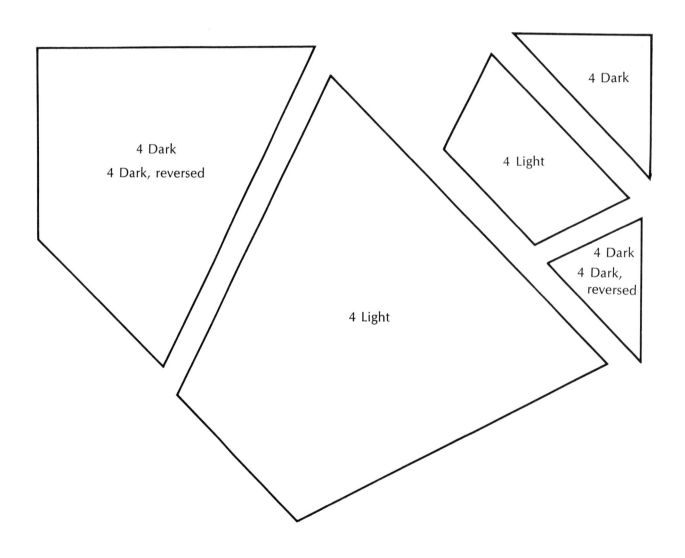

4 Dark
4 Dark, reversed

4 Light

4 Light

4 Dark

4 Dark
4 Dark,
reversed

Made of three colors, this is a very pretty design, and, I trust, will do credit to "Little Rhody." The quilt may be entirely of pieced work, or the blocks may be joined with plain strips or squares.
(Patience Pettigrew—Tiverton, R. I.)

Rhode Island

This quilt, measuring 88 x 100 inches, is made up of fifty-six 12-inch pieced blocks set seven in width and eight in length with a 2-inch dark border.

MATERIALS
Light, 6 yards
Medium, 3½ yards
Dark, 5 yards (includes border)

4 Medium

ALLOW FOR ALL SEAMS WHEN CUTTING

59

Continued on next page

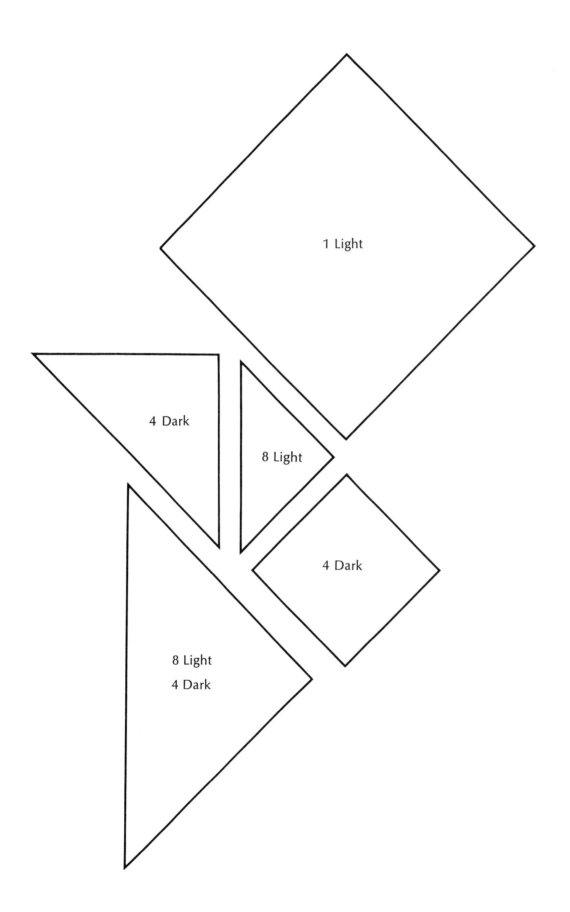

1 Light

4 Dark

8 Light

4 Dark

8 Light
4 Dark

While any quilt is, of course, prettier if pieced of uniform colors—two or three, as may be required— most housekeepers like to utilize small remnants left from the making of wash-dresses, such as percale, gingham, cambric, etc. When such scraps are used it is a good plan to arrange them as regularly as possible, which can be done with a little forethought; take care so that the colors which are brought together in one square are harmonious — one may secure artistic effects even in a patchwork quilt! Where cotton under-garments are made at home the pieces of bleached muslin or domestic will come in good play for white or light patches. The block illustrated is a desirable one for using small scraps; and the quilt may be entirely of pieced work, or joined with plain squares or strips, as preferred. (Judith B.)

South Carolina

This quilt, measuring 88 x 100 inches, is made up of fifty-six 12-inch blocks set seven in width and eight in length with a 2-inch dark border.

MATERIALS
Light, 3½ yards
Medium (or print), 4½ yards
Dark, 3½ yards (includes border)

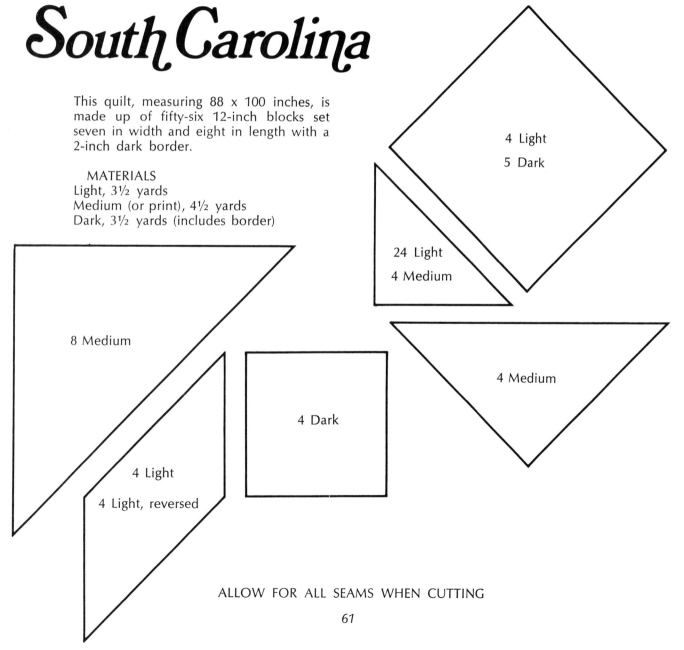

4 Light
5 Dark

24 Light
4 Medium

4 Medium

8 Medium

4 Light
4 Light, reversed

4 Dark

ALLOW FOR ALL SEAMS WHEN CUTTING

61

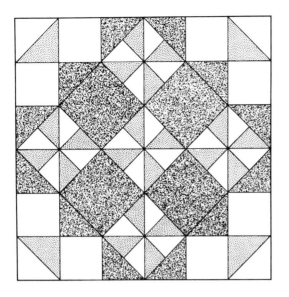

South Dakota

This quilt, measuring 78 x 93 inches, is made up of thirty 12-inch pieced blocks set five in width and six in length with 3-inch strips of light material set between the blocks. Add a 3-inch border of the light material and bind with the dark material.

MATERIALS
Light, 5 yards (includes strips and border)
Medium, 2 yards
Dark, 2¾ yards (includes binding)

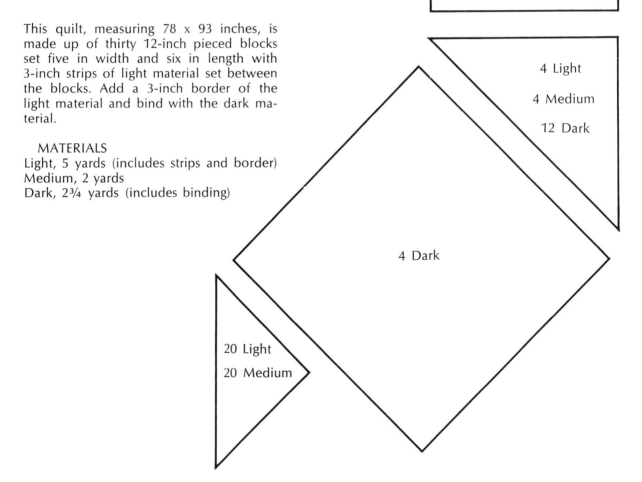

8 Light

4 Light
4 Medium
12 Dark

4 Dark

20 Light
20 Medium

ALLOW FOR ALL SEAMS WHEN CUTTING

Tennessee

This quilt, measuring 84 x 98 inches, is made up of forty-two 14-inch pieced blocks set six in width and seven in length. Bind with light material.

MATERIALS
Light, 6½ yards (includes binding)
Medium, 2½ yards
Dark, 3 yards

4 Light

8 Light
8 Medium
8 Dark

4 Light

ALLOW FOR ALL SEAMS WHEN CUTTING

Place on
fold of fabric

1 Medium

1 Dark

1 Medium

1 Dark

Place on
fold of fabric

This design is an original and represents the seal of the "Lone Star State." It may be pieced of red, white and blue, and the star may have a letter outlined in each point—T-E-X-A-S.

Texas

This quilt, measuring 84 x 108 inches, is made up of thirty-two 12-inch pieced blocks and thirty-one 12-inch plain blocks (cut 12½'') set alternately seven in width and nine in length. Bind with dark material.

MATERIALS
Light (or white), 8¾ yards (includes plain blocks)
Medium (or red), 2 yards
Dark (or blue), 2 yards (includes binding)

NOTE
Sew star together first. Then fill in points and add corners.

4 Medium

ALLOW FOR ALL SEAMS WHEN CUTTING

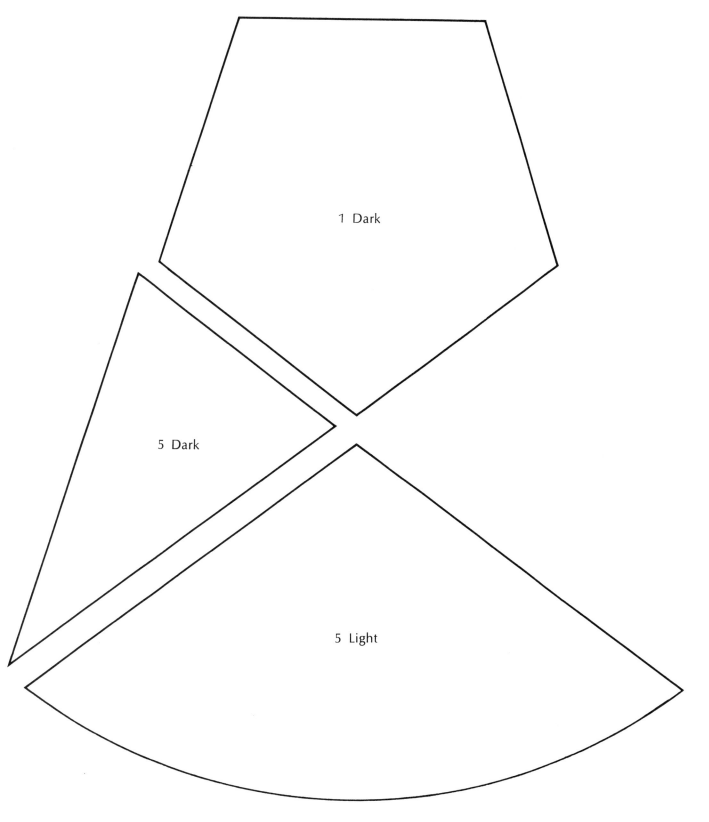

1 Dark

5 Dark

5 Light

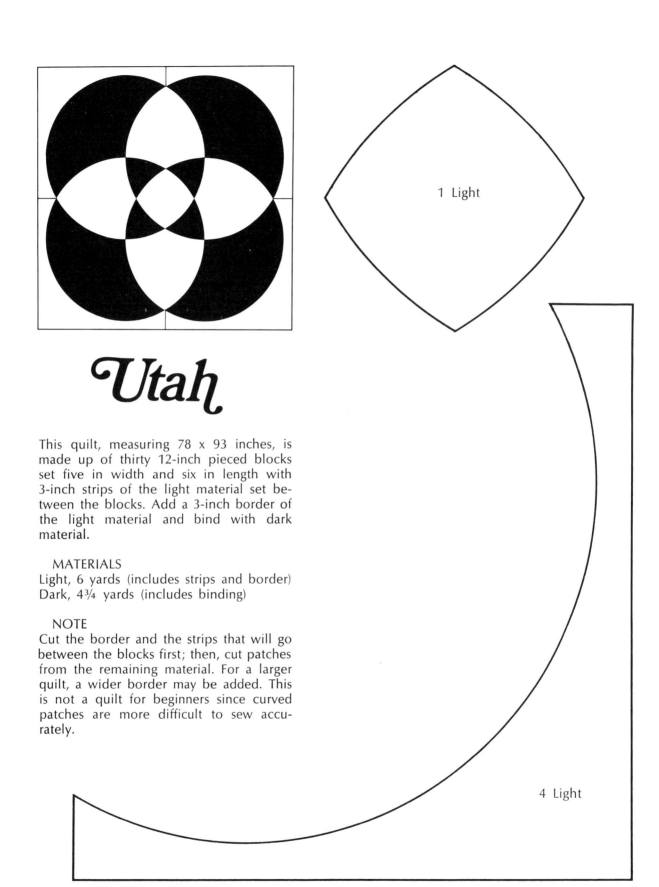

Utah

This quilt, measuring 78 x 93 inches, is made up of thirty 12-inch pieced blocks set five in width and six in length with 3-inch strips of the light material set between the blocks. Add a 3-inch border of the light material and bind with dark material.

MATERIALS
Light, 6 yards (includes strips and border)
Dark, 4¾ yards (includes binding)

NOTE
Cut the border and the strips that will go between the blocks first; then, cut patches from the remaining material. For a larger quilt, a wider border may be added. This is not a quilt for beginners since curved patches are more difficult to sew accurately.

1 Light

4 Light

ALLOW FOR ALL SEAMS WHEN CUTTING

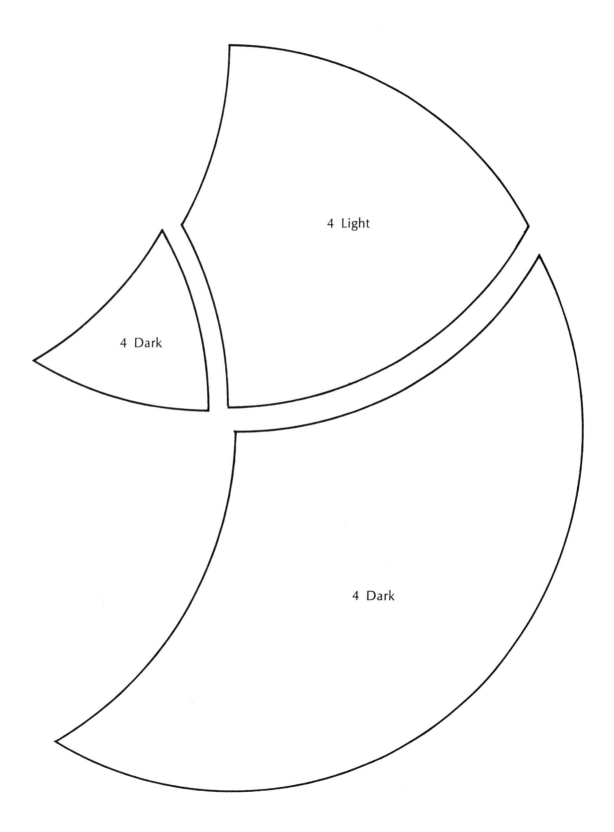

4 Light

4 Dark

4 Dark

Vermont

This quilt, measuring 84 x 96 inches, is made up of fifty-six 12-inch pieced blocks set seven in width and eight in length. Bind with dark material.

MATERIALS
Light, 4 yards
Medium, 5 yards
Dark, 4½ yards (includes binding)

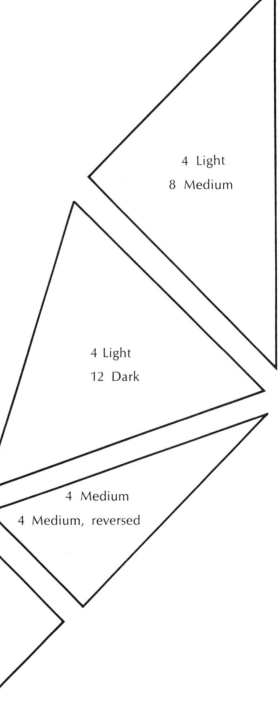

4 Light
8 Medium

4 Light
12 Dark

4 Medium
4 Medium, reversed

4 Light

ALLOW FOR ALL SEAMS WHEN CUTTING

Virginia

This quilt, measuring 84 x 96 inches, is made up of fifty-six 12-inch pieced blocks set seven in width and eight in length. Bind with dark fabric.

MATERIALS
Light, 3½ yards
Medium, 4½ yards
Dark, 2 yards

NOTE
Use medium and light fabric to piece together the center square as shown below.

4 Light

4 Medium

ALLOW FOR ALL SEAMS WHEN CUTTING

Continued on next page

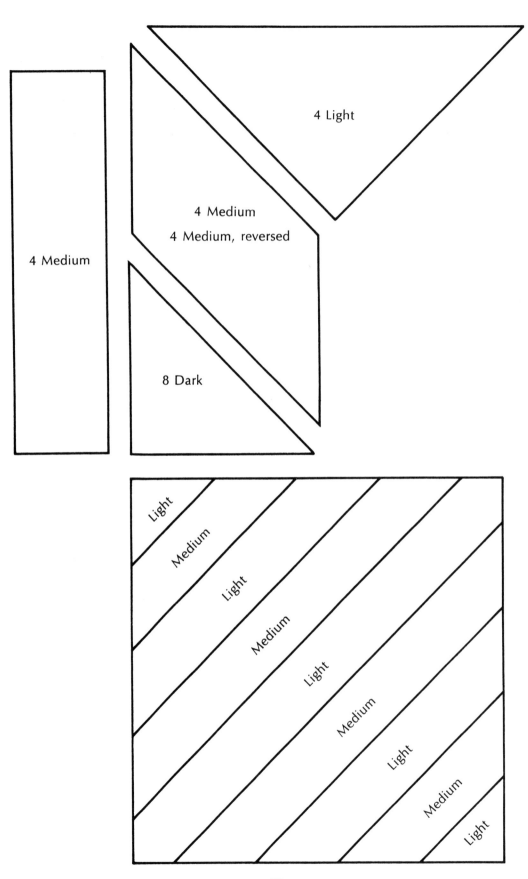

4 Light

4 Medium

4 Medium

4 Medium, reversed

8 Dark

Light

Medium

Light

Medium

Light

Medium

Light

Medium

Light

Washington

This quilt, measuring 84 x 108 inches, is made up of thirty-two 12-inch pieced blocks and thirty-one 12-inch plain blocks (cut 12½″) set alternately seven in width and nine in length. Bind with dark material.

MATERIALS
Light, 5½ yards (includes material for plain blocks)
Medium, 1½ yards
Dark, 4¾ yards (includes binding)

This is an admirable pattern for using small pieces, for which purpose it was originally designed. While any quilt is prettier if made of uniform colors, not all care to buy new goods to cut up, but prefer to utilize the accumulation of scraps from dresses and aprons of wash-goods. The pattern is also very pretty for an album-quilt, the name and address of the one contributing the block, being written on the white strips crossing the center. Join the quilt with plain squares of strips, or make it entirely of pieced blocks, as preferred. (Mrs. Abigail Boutwell Walker Karr)

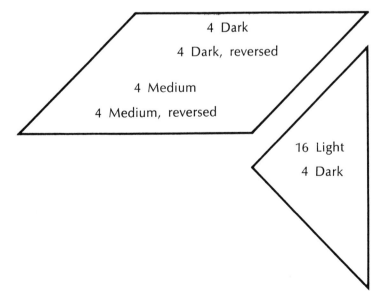

4 Light

4 Dark
4 Dark, reversed

4 Medium
4 Medium, reversed

16 Light
4 Dark

ALLOW FOR ALL SEAMS WHEN CUTTING

Continued on next page

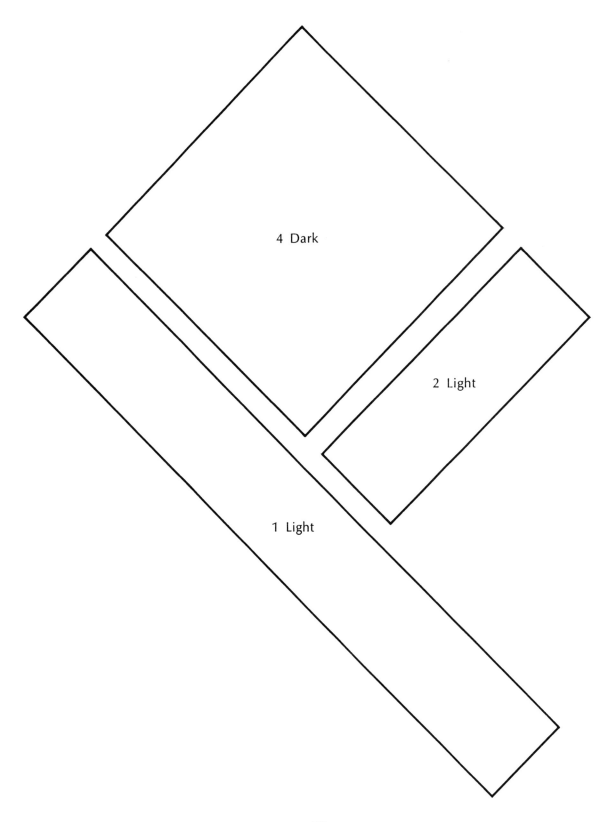

4 Dark

2 Light

1 Light

West Virginia

This quilt, measuring 78 x 91 inches, is made up of forty-two 13-inch pieced blocks set six in width and seven in length. The quilt may be bound with dark material.

MATERIALS
Light, 6½ yards
Medium, 2¼ yards
Dark, 2¼ yards (Add an additional ½ yard for binding)

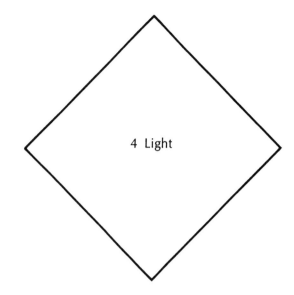

4 Light

12 Medium
12 Dark

8 Light

4 Light

Wisconsin

This quilt, measuring 88 x 100 inches, is made up of fifty-six 12-inch pieced blocks set seven in width and eight in length with a 2-inch dark border.

MATERIALS
Light, 7½ yards
Medium, 3½ yards
Dark, 4²/₃ yards (includes 2-inch border)

Three colors are used for this quilt, either the same throughout or remnants of dark, medium and light or white. The blocks may be joined throughout with plain squares or strips, or with half squares in the pretty zigzag or fence rail fashion; or the quilt will be very pretty made entirely of pieced blocks.

(Trixie Trix, Oshkosh, Wis.)

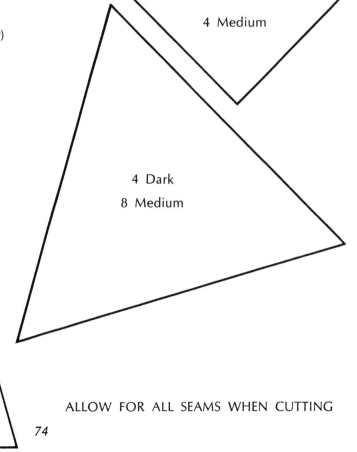

1 Dark

4 Medium

4 Dark
8 Medium

12 Light
4 Dark

4 Light

ALLOW FOR ALL SEAMS WHEN CUTTING

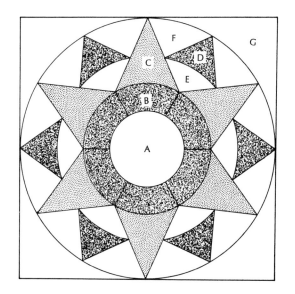

This is very pretty pieced of three colors—red, white and blue being especially pleasing. The design is original, and I had thought of calling it "Rolling Star." It makes a very desirable album or friendship block, the name and address of the one donating it, with any desired inscription, being written or outlined on the white circle in the center. (C. Helms)

Wyoming

This quilt, measuring 88 x 100 inches, is made up of twenty-eight 12-inch pieced blocks and twenty-eight 12-inch plain blocks (cut 12½") set alternately seven in width and eight in length. Finish with a 2-inch border of the dark fabric.

MATERIALS
Light (or white), 3½ yards (includes plain blocks)
Medium (or blue), 1 yard
Dark (or red), 3 yards (includes 2-inch border)

NOTE
Sew C to B and then sew this to A. Sew D to E; add F on each side and fill in points. Add corners.

F 6 Light

ALLOW FOR ALL SEAMS WHEN CUTTING

Continued on next page

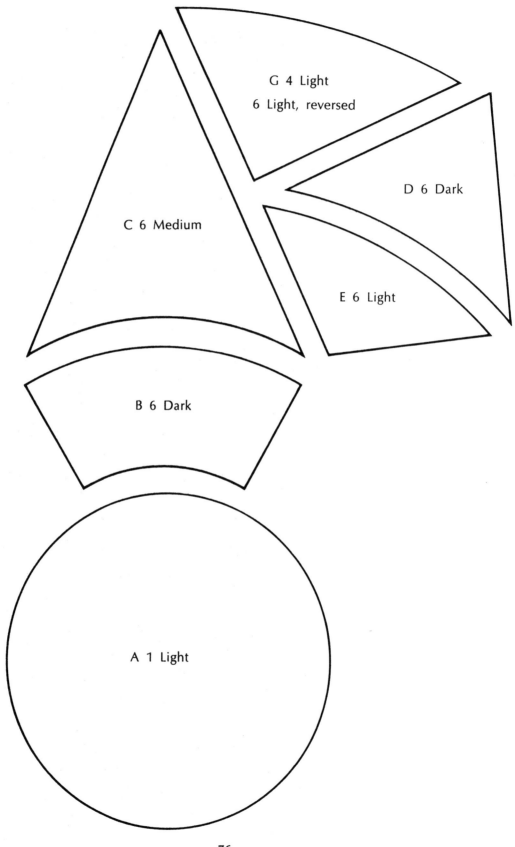

G 4 Light
6 Light, reversed

D 6 Dark

C 6 Medium

E 6 Light

B 6 Dark

A 1 Light